Congo Sole

Congo Sole

How a Once Barefoot Refugee Delivered Hope, Faith, and 20,000 Pairs of Shoes

EMMANUEL NTiBONERA
with DREW MENARD

NASHVILLE

NEW YORK • LONDON • MELBOURNE • VANCOUVER

Congo Sole
How a Once Barefoot Refugee Delivered Hope, Faith, and 20,000 Pairs of Shoes

© 2021 EMMANUEL NTIBONERA with DREW MENARD

Published in New York, New York, by Morgan James Publishing. Morgan James is a trademark of Morgan James, LLC. www.MorganJamesPublishing.com

List of Bible Translations used: NIV, NLT, NKJV, ESV

ISBN 978-1-64279-927-9 paperback
ISBN 978-1-64279-928-6 eBook
Library of Congress Control Number: 2019918457

Cover Design by:
Rachel Lopez
www.r2cdesign.com

Interior Design by:
Bonnie Bushman
The Whole Caboodle Graphic Design

Morgan James is a proud partner of Habitat for Humanity Peninsula and Greater Williamsburg. Partners in building since 2006.

Get involved today! Visit
www.MorganJamesBuilds.com

Table of Contents

Home, But Not Home
(Homecoming Part 1)
2015

For so much of my life, I had been running—running away from the Congo. Now, fifteen years later, here I was sweating under the hot African sun watching the customs officials' hands crawl slow like a chameleon across the keyboard as I waited to get back in.

The last time I was at this crossroads, the border between the Democratic Republic of the Congo and Rwanda, I was nationless—a refugee fleeing for my life. But the hot foil stamp embedded in the smooth cover of my brand-new U.S. passport says otherwise. I was part of a new nation now. A U.S. citizen at last. I gripped my passport tightly as I approached the armed border patrol with my dad and two of my brothers, John and Baraka. The stone-faced Rwandan guards stared daggers with rifles in hand. They don't trust Congolese; they're very strict, no-nonsense with my people. Only that little blue document protected me. Guns everywhere, tension in the air, but my passport commanded respect. Even with it, I still felt nervous—like the skin-and-bones boy who had barely made it across the border with his life not so long ago. I felt the stiff pages within the binding. It was just blue plastic, but to my former community, a collection of displaced outcasts and the forgotten still living in African refugee camps, it was a golden ticket.

In 2000, my family and I ran to escape the bloodshed and uncertainty of the Great War of Africa, which had plagued our homeland. The Second Congo War—Africa's World War—claimed over five million of my countrymen and has been called the bloodiest conflict since World War II.

Exiled in Kenya, we had no home, no work, and no way to provide for ourselves. To survive, I was told, "Keep moving forward. Don't look back." But the war haunted us every step of the way, stalking us like a leopard, waiting for us to wear down, give up, and return to her hungry jaws. Many who escaped with us said they would have rather gone back to die in their homeland than continue to face the hardships of refugee life.

Still, my parents never lost faith. They taught me and my siblings to pray—always pray—even when it felt like those prayers were as hollow as our dreams of a better life. As my heart thundered in my adolescent chest from fear of violence, and my stomach roared with pangs of hunger, my eyes remained fixed upon the road ahead and the hope of where it may lead. And time after time, when all seemed hopeless, God was there. He always came through.

As I watched the sun illuminate the Congolese horizon, I reflected on how far I'd come since then. It had been six years since my family and

I woke up each morning worrying if there would be food on the table or if we would be praying over empty plates, hoping for a miracle. My belly was full every day now; I'd forgotten the feelings of starvation, when my stomach was tearing in two. It had been so long since our daily prayers of thanks to God were because we had simply survived another day— having hidden all day under the table as soldiers banged down doors just up the street. Far behind me were the days when my family and I had considerable cause to complain about need, and yet, in the midst of the struggle, we held on to faith. In the U.S., we found peace.

In 2014, after nearly six years in the States, I'd built myself a comfortable life. While we attended Liberty University in Virginia, John, Baraka, and I lived in an apartment four times as large as the room I shared with my entire family in Kenya where we fled after we escaped the Congo. I studied health science and, in the evenings, I worked at school as a soccer referee for the university's intramurals. When Dad was a refugee he wasn't even allowed to work to provide for his family. We lived off faith. At Liberty, my job involved my favorite sport; the worst part about it was the ever-present urge to be a part of the action on the field. There was always something new to try at the dining hall—I'd developed a taste for lasagna—and, as long as I remembered to do my laundry, I had a fresh change of clothes every day.

My new reality, the life of excess I had been afforded, was why I made a trip to visit the Congo just months after officially becoming a U.S. citizen.

It struck me one day in the fall of 2014, sitting in a Convocation assembly at Liberty: *I wasn't running anymore.*

I liked to stand in the back of the service, so I could take in the whole atmosphere—thousands of people, young like me, in one place, raising their hands, singing with one voice, worshipping God. That particular morning, I could see the glowing faces of the other students as we heard about multiple mission trip opportunities. In front of me, a row of girls leaned over to one another, upperclassmen telling the younger students where they had gone before and why it was worth giving up a spring break to serve overseas. From the stage, we were being invited to serve in countries across Europe, Asia, even Africa. The scene of hip, young college students melted as faces flashed in my mind: family members left behind, friends from long ago. I could see their mouths, drawn tight, trying to look strong for their wide-eyed children, shaking with fear.

Images flashed on the giant screens across the vast arena—smiling students in bright red LU T-shirts hugging packs of little brown schoolchildren. Some of them were barefoot. I shifted on my feet, my black and white converse grazing the concrete concourse. John had on brown leather boots. I looked around and saw that everyone in that room had shoes on and I remembered that I did not own my first pair until I was ten-years-old. Just one pair of shoes had been a miracle. I knew my people were still suffering. *They should be going to the Congo*, I thought as I surveyed the arena.

Across the dim auditorium I watched the blue light bathe the faces of my classmates. They were glowing with the promise of a bright future, thanks to the freedom offered in the United States of America. Education is readily accessible. The biggest problem on most of our minds was passing the next test, getting enough credits to move on and chase our dreams. For me, it was wondering how fast I could get my homework done so that I could go play soccer with my friends.

But as far as I had run from my past, despite the ocean and thousands of miles, it still clung to me. I would wake in the middle of the night soaked in sweat from another nightmare. I hugged myself tighter under my covers as flashes of my youth passed before me. I could hear the sounds of gunshots echoing off the walls and women's screams ringing out. The worst sounds were the cries of abandoned children. *Mama! Mama!*—I got chills as their unanswered calls replayed in my head. I felt my bare feet throbbing against the hard ground as we ran, breathless.

I could still feel the sharp sting of the needle as Mom dug flesh-eating jiggers out of my calloused soles—a parasitic insect that still plagues those who cannot afford something as fundamental as shoes. And I saw my family—Mom and Dad pushing us forward as we tired out on the road out of Bukavu, never letting us fall behind among the sea of bodies looking to escape the attacks. Their love, their sacrifice for my family formed a bond in all of us that kept us alive.

For the first time in my life, I realized that I was truly safe; we were safe. God's hand had been on my family from the beginning, and He delivered us from certain death. But that day in the auditorium, as I listened to stories of my classmates aiding refugees in Greece (I had friends in the psychology program who went as a group there) or building a school in Rwanda—right next door to my motherland— God put his hand on my heart and breathed in me a purpose. After years of running, I finally understood why I had been so fortunate, why I had escaped. I could use my harrowing experiences as a war refugee to help others. I could be the miracle I so desperately needed as a boy. And I could rally others around the Congo. It was time to look back.

And then sitting there, looking at all my friends' feet, covered in sneakers in a rainbow of colors, it came to me: shoes.

A half a dozen or so pairs littered the floor of my room, not to mention the ones I'd left behind in my closet at my parents' new home in Greensboro, North Carolina. What was I doing with twelve pairs of shoes?

The next time I visited my parents, I started digging through my closet. There were some really good shoes in there that I didn't even wear anymore. I felt the rubber of the soles against my fingertips; the tread pattern glided across my skin with no resistance, hardly worn at all. I immediately pulled out a box and started collecting the discarded sneakers, beginning with my own. Then, I went through the rest of the house and gathered my family's neglected shoes. *Maybe*, I thought, *they could be put to good use.* I started asking my friends, everyone I came across, to contribute. There were kids in my motherland praying for a single pair of shoes. And the answers to those prayers were collecting dust in the back of American closets. Why waste a miracle?

As the pile of shoes in my room grew, so did my burden for my people. I officially became an American citizen on February 28, 2015. By July, I was watching my new country fade beneath a blanket of cloud as I journeyed back to the Congo.

We touched down at Kamembe International Airport in Rwanda and had to weave along five miles of road to get to the border. I hardly noticed the smooth pavement gliding beneath the tires as I looked out the taxi window. I'd see bustling marketplaces whiz by, followed by clusters of emerald trees. It was strange to be moving through Rwanda again. This time, instead of using it as a window of escape from the Congo, it was my doorway back in.

Our group passed from Rwanda into the Congo by way of the Rusizi International Bridge—we did so on foot while our taxi and the van with our luggage was searched and sent to meet us on the other side. If I shielded my eyes from the unrelenting sun, I could see in the distance new structures rising above the sprawling city of Bukavu, my hometown—colorful buildings built into the sides of the steep hills that frame the water below. I did not recognize them. I wondered if my people, like their neighboring Rwandans, had managed to rebuild their lives and find peace in the aftermath of the war.

But just steps over the border it was obvious that there was a world of difference between the neighboring nations of Congo and Rwanda— it was even evident in the roads. The moment our taxi took off on the Congolese side, my body was jerked about as the vehicle rattled into Bukavu. Garbage lined the dirt streets, like a raw, festering wound. With each bump, I felt as if the scars from the war that had driven me out were still fresh. The anticipation that I felt crossing over the bridge into my motherland evaporated as I looked around me, replaced with a sense of despair.

I was not prepared for what was ahead of me. The war may have been over, but the suffering was not. This was my home but yet it wasn't—not like I had remembered it. Hotels stood upright, freshly painted in pastel colors, but directly across the street were ramshackle homes made of rusty metal, falling apart on top of one another. Some looked like they had been made from mud. Filth piled in the ditches; when it rained, waste snaked through the muddy runs along the roads until it clogged up, forming heaps of soggy trash.

The air was hot and thick when I arrived at my hotel. As I stepped out onto Congolese ground, I could feel the hard-packed soil through the soles of my white high-top Nike Air Force 1s, firm and unforgiving. The soil was brown, but in my mind's eye it was still red with blood from those slaughtered not but a decade ago. I grimaced as dust smeared across my once-immaculate shoes. *How could so much time have passed yet so little had changed?* I had to see more, so I hurried my father and brothers as we dropped our belongings at the hotel. We set out in search of something, anything, familiar.

The wounds of war were far deeper than I had imagined. The devastation only got worse as I ventured deeper into Bukavu's neighborhoods, once my stomping grounds. Overpopulation now suffocated my city. The summer heat baked the garbage piles, filling the air with a lingering stench as I walked the very streets that I had played on as a child, kicking soccer balls made of wadded-up plastic shopping bags and dancing until Mom called us home for a fresh meal. The sturdy homes I remembered were run down, and shacks were propped up against them. The streets were narrower than I remembered. Houses pressed in on each side, squeezing the traffic so that when cars zipped by, not minding the pedestrians, their tires rolled inches from your toes as you tried to move out of the way. Blinking dust out of my eyes, I sighed when I saw that the wide, open parks where I used to run carefree with John by my side and Baraka chasing after, had been swallowed up, every inch of breathable space choked out by makeshift shelters.

I reconnected with friends and family. The ones we'd managed to keep up with across the distance helped us find others we had no idea were still alive. I saw new lines in faces I had known as a child. Others I hardly recognized at all. And there were new faces, cousins I had never even met. But they were a part of me—we were all born out of Congo's violent history. Our parents may have given us similar noses, eyes, mouths, the same dark skin, but the conflict had molded us, hardened us. A legacy not of genes, but of survival.

There were faces unaccounted for, too. Many were murdered, their bodies strewn on blood-soaked sheets, right in their own homes. Parents slaughtered in front of their children—my old playmates. Some vanished with no word. I can only imagine what fate—what horrors—they may have endured, and I hoped beyond hope they had escaped.

I felt the weight of these losses, not in the textures of the city—the course brick, the uneven dirt—but in the space that filled the gaps where my friends should have been to greet me.

Around me, children still played together, laughing, yelling, running, and completely ignorant of their bleak living conditions. Kids will always be kids. Adults leaned in groups against cracked stonewalls, smiles stretched across their faces as they passed away the time. I'd see them break out into song and dance—just like my friends and I used to—clapping a thunderous rhythm beneath a joyful chorus.

But I looked closer and saw kids' bones poking against their skin. They felt like walking skeletons as they brushed past me in the narrow streets. Their tattered clothes flapped loosely against their skinny frames. You could almost taste the lingering odor from the fabrics, over-worn but still holding stubbornly together. Weary-eyed mothers peeked out at me from behind ragged curtains draped over otherwise bare doorways.

My people remained positive, though. Happy and ready to talk your ear off, just like I remembered. But the pain was deep, just beneath the surface. When I spoke to people, they would tell me they were thankful for today's meal, even if they weren't sure if there would be one tomorrow. They were taking life one day at a time.

I suddenly realized that the collection of shoes I had started back home in the United States—boxes of scuffed trainers billowing out across my room—seemed so small compared to the crowds of villagers who now sought refuge in the crumbling concrete jungle. The extent of the need was so much greater than I anticipated. These people—my people—needed a miracle.

My heart ached and I longed for the Congo of my youth. We may not have had many earthly possessions, but it was a good life. Carefree. Before everything changed. Before the terror and before the running.

I stood in the center of the road, my shoes now completely covered in dirt, and stilled my mind to pray. *Breathe in. Breathe out.* The soundtrack of my past rang silent in the air. I could feel these people's pain, because I had felt it, too. I knew these horrors were behind me, but the things I heard as a young boy haunt me still. I prayed to myself, *Lord, bless them as I have been blessed. And bless me more, so that I can give back.*

I had returned to my motherland as a man, equipped with my faith, my God-given purpose, and my family by my side. Together, with those tools, we would aim to lift up the Congolese people and place them securely on their feet. I knew that with my ambition and my growing collection of donated shoes in the U.S. that we had the potential to change the course of a few peoples' lives. I just wasn't expecting the Congo to alter my life forever. Again.

Chapter One

Dancing in the Streets
1986-1995

When I was a child—before the war, before the killing, before the running—survival was not the driving force of my life. I was a normal kid: I went to school, played with my friends, ate dinner every evening with my family, and went to church on Sundays. I had aspirations—to become a famous singer—and dreams of what my life would become.

My family enjoyed a good life. We lived in a seven-bedroom house, which was part of a larger compound my dad owned, which he rented out. Dad also owned some businesses, including the community's supermarket.

Our red-brick house had a large dirt yard with some wild shrubs. Sometimes the rains would soak the ground so much that our feet would get sucked into the mud as we tried to run and play soccer. That didn't stop me and John or our friends from enjoying ourselves. We loved playing in the mud, getting caked with the stuff as we molded houses and other creations in the earth like Play-Dough. We didn't have toys like American children, but in our simple life we had plenty of fun. When it was dry, we'd set up two stones on each side of the yard as soccer goals and wear ourselves out kicking the homemade ball, running around after one another in a large pack trying to score goals.

Life in my old neighborhood embodied what it means to be a community. We didn't lock ourselves in our own spaces, walled off from our neighbors. Congolese people are very close; we all lived like one big family.

Whenever someone would slaughter a cow, everyone in the neighborhood got a piece. You didn't even have to ask—you would just walk right up and they would give you a share. People wanted their neighbors to enjoy the food alongside them after they'd taken time to prepare a special meal, like roasted goat or fresh fish caught right from the lake with rice and sweet potatoes. But Congolese were, and are to this day, just as quick to share a small pot of rice and beans if they knew you were hungry. We looked out for each other.

There was an understanding among the adults in the community that if they caught any of us kids acting out that they could deal with us themselves and not wait to tell our parents. We were taught to always respect our elders. So, when we got out of line, testing boundaries as we navigated the busy streets chasing and yelling after one another, it was worse to be caught by my friend's mother. She'd set me straight with a stern talking, or even a smack, and then I'd get another at home from my own mother. News traveled fast.

But when I'd scrape my elbow after cutting a corner too fast in a narrow alleyway or skin my knee raw on a rocky field, that same friend's mother would be just as quick to clean up my cuts and send me home where I knew Mom would have a kiss waiting for me.

It was not uncommon for me to walk into my house and find people I didn't even know sitting around the table with my parents. They loved to entertain and extended hospitality to anyone they met.

When I first came to the U.S., I was met with scowls just for waving *Hi* to the other tenants in the apartment complex my family was brought to. While I've made many friends since then, I still often miss the communal bond of Congolese life.

Walking was a big part of our daily lives. My siblings and I walked to school six days a week—it started at 7 a.m. and lasted until 1:45 in the afternoon. And it was a good hour's walk to school each morning, so we had to get up with the sun.

We also didn't have indoor plumbing. Our house had a large, black plastic drum that filled up with water as it rained. But in the dry season it fell on me, as the oldest child, to walk forty-five minutes to the nearest well to collect water, which we used for cooking, drinking, and washing. I would have to carry the water in a plastic jug balanced on my head. When it was full, I felt shorter as the weight of the water pressed down, forcing me to hunch forward as I walked, water splashing the dirt into clay around my feet. You didn't want to lose too much; it took about four or five trips to fill up the tank already. But in the hot weather, I admit I didn't mind when it would occasionally spill over onto my shirt.

My friends and I usually all went together since it was the boys' job to fetch the water, for the most part. This made the trips a little better. Sometimes even fun. We'd groan when we'd arrive at the well and there was a long line. But then we'd set our jugs down to claim a spot and go off and play soccer, darting back and forth between the field and the row of people to kick the containers forward, keeping our places.

Sunday was our only day off from school, chores, and other responsibilities. My father was a Pentecostal preacher. The Word was his true calling—he loved to preach, and people loved to listen. So, we never missed church—which went from 10 a.m. until 4 p.m. That was especially difficult for me as a kid—all I wanted to do was get out, run, have adventures, and perform my music. John and I were in the youth choir, which I always looked forward to. It left a lasting impact on my heart, even if I didn't know it at the time. It was there that our musical talents flourished.

Before the rebels (both homegrown insurgents and illegal foreign armed troops) invaded our cities and many young boys disappeared—forced to march, carry guns, and kill—children roamed the streets of Bukavu unsupervised, carefree, happy. My little brother, John, and I, only a year apart, were inseparable. We used to gather our friends from around the neighborhood and put on concerts along the main road through the crowded marketplace.

There was a flat, dirt bank that rose about three feet above the road, held in place by a low brick wall. Up there, we could practically taste the fresh goat and fowl roasting in nearby restaurants and look down on our unaware concert attendees. Bodies squeezed past one another as buyers and sellers weaved up and down the wide, unpaved street, their footprints hammering the ground flat. Old ladies, faces leathered by years in the sun, propped boards on buckets in their laps to display slabs of raw meat. Traditional clothing billowed over carts, the intricate, geometric patterns over vibrant fabrics flashing through the constant flow of bodies. Children craned their necks to see past the women balancing buckets of dried beans on their heads, wrapped in colorful scarves.

Every couple of weeks, my friends and I would put on a show for them from our roadside stage. We'd bang a heavy rhythm using buckets and cut-up tire tubes stretched over cans for drums. If we didn't have anything to drum, we'd stomp our feet, spraying earth as we sang out, our voices carrying above the noise of the crowd. Sometimes we danced along to the radio. As a song would build, John—always front and center—would scurry up a tree. He'd cue a drumroll and vault down to the ground, like we were in a music video, giving even the fish merchants up the road something to see. Then, he'd sing the next line of the verse at the top of his lungs, drawing even more onlookers.

The music was fast and upbeat: Congolese *seben*. Think reggae and rumba flavors: smooth, heavy rhythms with playful, high melodies, fast and airy. Each song was like a celebration, the vocals echoing out in dramatic layers, anchored by group harmony. Crowds would form and cheer us on, shouting back their responses to our vocal calls and swaying to the beat.

As we danced, John did somersaults and high-flying kicks, his feet light and quick as lightning. Sweat would rain on the ground as our bodies moved in time. We'd go on for hours, until we ran out of breath, our legs melting and muscles on fire.

There were stars in our eyes. I dreamed that one day I'd be recruited to join a large band and travel the country. People would know my name; they'd clap and cheer and sing along wherever I went. I suppose that is not so different from what many American children dream of.

When I got home, sweat pouring down my face, I'd find Mom outside over the open fire stove, humming hymns to herself as she prepared dinner. My belly would growl as I sniffed the air, my nose tasting the simmering beef stew or pan-fried fish before my mouth got the chance.

There were many times when my appetite would have to wait, though. If my parents caught us dozing too much during our nightly devotions, they'd start to make us do them before dinner. Dad would bring out his black, leather-bound Bible, lick his fingers, and snap the crisp pages back and forth. He knew that book inside and out and took great care of it. Dad has that same Bible to this day, and it looks as good as new. Even though I would look over my shoulder as my mouth watered for the meal just waiting to be devoured, I know that it was these moments where I learned to be a man. Dad's deep voice, which thundered to the back wall of the church, would take a more tender tone as our family circled around the table.

During devotions, Dad liked to croon *nyimbo za wokovu*: Congolese salvation songs. He had a book full of them. Some songs he wrote himself, scribbled in a small leather notebook. The rest of the family would join in, adding harmony, our voices blending perfectly together. I remember the way Mom's sweet voice would melt right in with ours. We'd all take turns leading the singing, us kids getting to choose our favorite contemporary praise and worship songs. All of my siblings have developed a passion for music, and it started at home.

God used my parents' love of music to bring them together in 1986, when my dad, Vincent Ntibonera, met my mom, Martha, in the church choir.

They married in 1987, and Psalm 128:3 was read during the ceremony: "Your wife will be like a fruitful vine within your house, your children will be like olive shoots around your table" (NIV). In the Congo, a large family is a sign of blessing and prosperity. So, my parents were thrilled when they found out just months after the wedding that they were going to have a child. Their firstborn—was a boy. Oh, what hope they must have felt as new parents for the future of their family, for they named my older brother Ojenge, which means, "to build."

But I never got to meet him. After only twelve months, Ojenge became suddenly ill with Malaria. For days, his fever spiked. Mom stayed up late into the night holding her precious baby as he shivered and cried. But there was nothing she could do, and Ojenge died.

My mother fell into despair. The excitement of becoming a new parent shattered, and Mom spent every night after Ojenge's passing crying herself to sleep. She was inconsolable. Though her little building block had been taken, the bedrock of Mom's life, family, and faith was not shaken. Mom did not turn her back on God. The resilient faith that she modeled to me as I suffered from malnutrition as a refugee years later was forged in those early days of motherhood. And though she prayed through the anguish, she wondered if she would ever be able to have more children of her own.

God heard Mom's cries and sent his hand down to comfort her. One day, sitting at home, she heard a knock at the door. Mom has retold the story to me dozens of times as a child, by my bedside or during family prayers. She opened the door to find a mysterious woman wearing a patterned green dress, hair hidden beneath the wrap that wove around her head.

Her heart heavy, Mom offered the best smile she could muster and welcomed the surprise guest inside. Mom was always hospitable to strangers. What the woman had to say flooded the darkened corners of my mom's anguished spirit with new light. "I have been sent by God to tell you to stop crying," the woman said. "He has heard your cry, and he told me to let you know that you will conceive again."

Mom's breath caught in her throat as her very fears were laid bare and stripped of their power.

"Your womb is blessed," the mysterious woman said with authority. "There are men and women in that womb. Soon, you will give birth to a baby boy, and his name will be 'Imani.'"

In English, the name—my name—means faith.

Immediately, the weight on Mom's heart released and she was filled with hope. She believed. Her spirit lifted. And from then on, she did not cry anymore. Mom never saw or heard from that woman again, but two months later, she discovered that she was pregnant. Miracles paved the road for my family. Looking back, I guess it really is no surprise that I came into this world as a miracle.

I was born almost exactly nine months later on April 27, 1989, and my parents named me just as the woman had foretold—Imani Nshokano Ntibonera. I was a consolation to Mom and Dad after the tragedy. Our family, like the blessed vine in the Bible verse from my parents' wedding, began to grow and flourish and blossom before their eyes. A year after I was born, my brother John (Biranganine) was born, followed another year later by Baraka (Zihalirwa), and then Christian (Agano) in 1994. Mother conceived, carried, and delivered five boys, and that was only the start. Over the next eight years she would bring five more children into our family, this time all girls—Danielle (Adili) in 1995, Priscilla (Kujirabwinja) in 1997, Asikiya "Asi" (Zihalirwa) in 1998, Naomi (Bachigale) in 2000, and Esther (Ebenezer) in 2003.

I remember clearly the Congo of my childhood. There was peace then. President Mobutu Sese Seko had been in power for decades, his regime able to quell the small coups that had threatened it. And, while his regime did not bring much prosperity to the nation (called the Republic of Zaire back then), there was a semblance of stability[1]. My motherland is an expansive nation. With a surface area of about one-and-a-half million miles, it lands just outside the top ten largest countries in the world[2], and its population is over eighty-one million[3], placing it in the top twenty most populated countries. And while the land is very rich in minerals—cobalt, coltan, copper, gold, diamonds, uranium, and zinc—to this day the DRC remains one of the least developed countries in the world[4].

Bukavu sits just beyond dense, green jungles. Located on the far Eastern edge of Congo, the city is right on the border of Rwanda. As a kid I would climb a tree, banana leaves fanning below me in the breeze, and see how the sun, hot in the sky, would glisten off of Lake Kivu, sending gold and blue waves rippling between our neighboring nations. It was such a beautiful country before the great war cast its shadow across my motherland.

Almost everyone carries around a piece of the Congo in their pocket because coltan is used in mobile phones and other electronic gadgets[5]. Our riches, however, have historically not been used for the benefit of our people. In the late 1800s, Belgians enslaved Congolese men in their own country to harvest rubber[6]. White settlers and the slave trade were, in later years, traded for warlords and dictators—centuries of people seeking to plunder and profit off the backs of Congolese. Despite our country's natural wealth, to this day the DRC remains one of the least developed countries in the world.

My father was also a businessman—he rented a convenience store-sized building at the market where he sold dry goods in large quantities—and he first tasted the conflict that would soon plague our country while on a business trip. I was about four years old at the time.

Dad and a group of six other men, including his business partner, were driving a truck down a rural road when bullets whizzed past their vehicle. The driver slammed on the brakes, bringing the car to a jarring halt. Armed militants—the sort of rogues who still infest the Eastern Congo, fighting for control over a region's people and resources—pulled up beside my dad and his friends and ordered them to get out of the truck and line up in the grass by the side of the road. Dad kept his hands up, not even daring to wipe the sweat pouring from his brow, as he followed their orders. There had been whispers from our friends and neighbors of armed robberies happening on back roads, but Dad never expected it to come this close to home. All that was on his mind was his wife and three boys back home.

The militants were on edge; many were pacing back and forth or adjusting the weapons slung over their shoulders. Then, without warning, a shot erupted, its deafening *crack* so loud Dad believed the bullet had struck him. He collapsed, hitting the ground alongside his partner, who had received the shot directly in the chest. Dad could hear another man begin to sob, pleading for his life. The distraction drew the attention of the highwaymen long enough for Dad to realize that he had not been hit. As blood pooled around him, hot and sticky, he fought to still his breathing despite the thunder in his chest. Shots continued to ring out, but Dad did not flinch, even as he heard bullets pound flesh, killing three more of his friends. He just played dead. Dad's mind raced, but his spirit held fast as he prayed silently. Though he wanted nothing more than to see his family again, Dad asked only for God's will to be done.

God's hand must have been on Dad, because the armed men robbed the two remaining captives but did not once lay a hand on him, though Dad had money in his pocket. Satisfied that they'd taken all they could, the robbers left. Dad was too terrified to move, afraid that the men might return to find survivors and finish them off. So, he and the others waited. An hour passed. Then another. Only after they were certain the attackers weren't coming back did the group feel safe enough to move from their lifeless positions. Instead of coming straight home after his near-death experience, Dad and his business partners decided to continue on and complete their work. I would see that same strength and resilience anchor our family in faith through our darkest days. Just a few months after Dad's hijacking, my childhood innocence would shatter. But even so, from the very beginning, God was watching over my family.

Chapter Two

The Thunder of War
1996

I t could have been a perfect day. The afternoon sun had withheld some of its strength so that we could run around all afternoon without our lungs withering and mouths drying up like deserts.

The fraying soccer ball kicked up dust as it rolled across the field behind my house, about fourteen of us boys fighting for possession, our bare feet thumping hard against the rubber. Even though the ball was wearing out, looking more tan than white now, it was still better than a homemade one—my friends and I had saved up the coins we collected performing at the marketplace to buy it.

John and I weaved the ball back and forth, reading each other's movements and cutting passes through the forest of limbs. We'd cheer as the spinning checkers finally sailed through the netless metal frame at the end of the field.

Baraka chased after us, trying to get in on the action. We would let him dribble through us as we towered over him. He'd run around and we would humor him with gentle passes as we caught our breath. (Today he's the best player of us all.) But the air was warm and crisp—it wasn't long before the game would intensify once again, and I'd tell Baraka to move over to the side so that he didn't get trampled.

As the sun started to go down, we began hearing pops in the distance. We were too focused on the game to worry at first. But the sounds persisted, growing louder and more frequent. I stopped to listen. The sky was clear and blue. There were only a few fluffy clouds scattered above as I tilted an ear up. More sounds echoed like thunder in the distance. I had heard about rebels in the jungle, rumors that war would come, but I never took it seriously—I was only seven. It wasn't real to me. Now, it was.

We tried to keep our game going—maybe we thought if we went on as normal that life would stay as it was—but by six o' clock, the rhythmic cracks of gunshots rang loud and constant. People began running through the streets in a wild frenzy to get home before the sounds reached them. I couldn't focus on what my feet were doing, I stopped playing and just stood, watching as people sprinted to the market to stock up on food or ran inside, slamming their doors behind them. The soccer ball sat untouched at our feet, out of mind. Parents started running to the field, yelling with urgency for my friends to get inside.

At first, as the violent sounds ripped through the air and crowds scrambled in chaos, I was thrown into confusion. I froze, heart racing, afraid that the earth would just open up and swallow me alive. I was like a statue, eyes glued ahead, until a familiar baritone cut through the madness. Dad's voice, calling me to get on inside with John and Baraka, snapped me back to reality. Grabbing a brother's hand in each of mine, I rushed across the field to my house, almost dragging Baraka as we ran. We didn't stop to pick up our ball.

By the time I burst through the door, fear had washed over me worse than the sweat binding my chest to my shirt. My eyes were wide, darting from left to right, searching out the windows for a sign of what was going on. In the distance, I watched smoke billowing from houses built into the mountain that looked down on us. I was just a child, my whole life ahead of me, but my mortality hit me like a brick as I saw the black cloud stain the horizon like spilled ink. I slammed the door and threw myself under the table.

John and Baraka scrambled to my parents' room and hid under the bed. Christian chased after them, laughing. He thought it was a game of hide-and-seek. The older boys tried to keep him still and quiet in between them on the floor.

Mom was preparing dinner outside when we got home. She heard us barge in and looked around her to see our neighbors barricading themselves inside. Shots continued to echo overhead. She dropped what she was doing, leaving the food while she rushed inside to take care of us children. Adili started crying. Mom scooped her up, drawing my sister close against her chest, tiny legs gripping around her pregnant belly. I couldn't understand the words from where I was in the house, but I heard Mom's soft, nurturing voice whispering to Adili. The sound comforted me as well.

Dad could not keep still. He kept pacing from room to room, checking and rechecking that everyone was inside and that the doors were locked and the shutters firmly clasped. He held his lips in a tight line. Dad was trying to keep a calm face for us, but I could see the worry clouding his eyes. He barricaded the door with some furniture and told us to not turn on any lights. No one should know anyone was home. The last golden beams had just begun to fade from the bottom slats of the shutters.

Under the large table, which was in the living room, I hugged my legs to my chest, fighting my rapid breathing, trying to be quiet. My heart beat so hard and fast I was sure that it could be heard outside. I leaned back against a table leg, the weight of the dark wood firm against my spine. Outside, the shots cracked, one after the other, a steady stream of bullets tearing apart the peaceful fabric of the city. The noise became so constant that I almost got used to it. Almost. When a neighbor would slam their door and rattle their locks, I'd jump with fear; I thought someone was kicking down our door. Afraid to leave the comfort of my wooden shelter, I'd crawl to the opposite end of the table, away from the direction of the noise. When I'd hear another bang from another neighbor locking up, I would slide over to a new spot. I kept shifting from table leg to table leg; every bump and clatter triggered the fear that bad men had arrived to kill my family.

There was a crackle of static in the living room as Dad tuned in his portable radio. Not willing to risk raising the volume for fear it would signal that someone was home, Dad pressed the device against his ear and listened. When he wasn't patrolling the house or whispering words of comfort to us, I'd see him hunched in a corner of the living room, grasping his chin in one fist, face scrunched, holding the radio up to his head in the other hand as the news trickled over the airwaves. The city was in chaos. The only message he clearly heard was that no one should be seen outside.

As darkness swept over the city, the neighborhood grew still. There was an uneasy tension between the eerie silence and the violent eruptions. I tried to tell myself the gunshots weren't getting any closer, but my mind didn't cooperate. In the blackness, I couldn't even see my hand in front of my face. I was so afraid to breathe. This was one of the first times I remember, on my own, truly thinking about what I believe. In that moment, I knew God was real; I could feel Him stirring in my soul. The still small voice was telling me not to fear, even though I did.

Mom snuck out to the outdoor kitchen, carrying Adili, who refused to be put down. She only had to take a few steps from the house to retrieve the food. I bit my lip as she took each one, afraid the bad men might see her.

Mom wouldn't dare light a fire to finish cooking, but she made sure each of us had something to eat. I wasn't hungry. My stomach was in knots. I still managed a few bites of something cold and forced it down my throat. I was so on edge that the food stuck before sliding down.

That night, just like they always did, Mom and Dad gathered the family together to pray. They crept through the house, calling us softly. We huddled close in a circle on the cold living room floor, hands clasped tightly together. Though this was the most terrifying night of my life, my earthly father showed strength I did not quite comprehend, confidently declaring that our Heavenly Father would be able to protect us. Dad said he could not keep all of us safe, but he promised that God was watching over us. If we stayed inside the house, Dad assured us no one would die there that night.

Mom lit a kerosene lamp, keeping it as dim as it could be. Through the orange light I saw my family wrapped in shadows. Only Mom and Dad closed their eyes when we prayed. Their words flowed out in delicate waves, washing a bit of relief over me. I could barely form words when I tried to pray out loud. They caught in my throat. Only brief phrases, "God deliver us," escaped my lips. And it was only in a hoarse whisper.

I felt better after drawing from my parents' strength. They kept their voices low, but they resounded with authority as they prayed. I was reminded where the source of their strength truly laid.

We went to bed after praying for more than an hour, but I couldn't sleep. My brothers and I shared a room. No one wanted to be alone in his or her bed with the thunder of war rippling across the night. The walls gave no comfort in the dark. So, John, Baraka, and Christian crawled into bed with me. Christian soon passed out against my chest; I felt his breathing ease as he drifted off. The rest of us laid there, afraid to even close our eyes. No words passed between us. We just took comfort knowing that if anything happened, we'd be together.

Early in the morning, Dad ordered us to start packing. He told us that he'd heard an announcement on the radio warning people to evacuate the city. Mom, seven months pregnant, shuffled from room to room, digging through drawers to find warm clothes for each of us. Her stomach looked like it would burst any moment. None of us could get her to be still; she just kept on going.

My eyes burned from exhaustion, but I was ready to get out of Bukavu. For Dad, it wasn't as simple as that. I would look out the window, straining my eyes against the sun, and watch my neighbors throwing bags over their shoulders and buckets on their heads, spilling grains of rice in the dust as they hurried out of town. I'd start nagging Dad, "When are we going to go?" But he just sat quietly, stroking his chin, deep in thought. My brothers and I would press on, our bodies fidgeting, "Let's go! Let's go!" He'd reassure us that we would leave when the time was right. He just wanted to make sure it was safe for all of us.

As more people zipped by the window, my brothers and I grew more impatient. Dad watched us with heavy eyes and then looked over at Mom, rationing the last of our food from the cupboards, Adili between her knees. My sister could barely walk, but she followed Mom across the house and back all day. Dad told us that it was important we all stay together. Then he went back to his thoughts, planning our best route for escape.

Time dragged as the day wore on. Outside, the city was turning into a war zone. Explosions rippled through the air from just beyond the city, and the gunfire never stopped. Almost everyone around us had left by mid-afternoon. The streets—once filled with mothers washing clothes in buckets and kids running after chickens—were empty, trampled until they were left lifeless. We were being left behind. I felt as if our house was shrinking around me. Suffocating, I kept checking the windows. All I could see beyond the quiet complex were rising plumes of charcoal, more smoke than the day before.

A group of my cousins—five of them, all in their twenties—came banging at the door around three p.m. All of them were armed, machetes gleaming off the sun as they entered the doorway, knives hanging off their belts. One of them carried a slasher—a reaping scythe for clearing away thick grass. The bitter scent of their sweat filled the house. My eyes expanded as I observed their weapons.

One of my cousins, Safari, leaned over to John and me, his large coat engulfing his thin frame. Hands rested on bent knees, he looked us in the eye and told us that we needed to be able to protect ourselves. He held up his machete, rust-spotted from use. Safari told us to search the house for knives, tools—anything we could use as a weapon. We took off, about to tear through the house when Dad froze us in our steps: "No." His tone was calm and even. But I still caught the firmness in his voice. He said no son of his was going to carry a weapon.

Safari, standing upright, nearly a head taller than Dad, urged him to gather the family and flee the city with his group. Dad sighed and shook his head. He said that it was not safe for our family to be in the streets. Not with so many little ones. I didn't see any point in staying and protested, telling him that John, Baraka, and I wanted to go on our own.

At the time, I didn't know that children were being recruited by the militias, often against their will. Dad was not willing to risk that or worse for us. He told us, once again, that we needed to stay together as a family.

Safari and my other cousins left as quickly as they had come. They said time was running out; rebels had already taken over much of the surrounding areas. I watched them disappear back into Bukavu, weapons tight in their hands, heads swiveling in search of danger. Our time was running out, I feared.

Dad called us over, kneeling so that we could look him directly in the eye. He looked tired, and he spoke slowly. He explained that he was doing what he thought was best to keep the family safe. He said we didn't need weapons—God was able to protect us. His inflection raised, unleashing the power of his conviction and the seriousness of our situation. Dad did not have the strength to keep us all alive, he said. If we were going to die, we would die as a family. But he knew God was on our side.

That night, as Mom arched her back to ease the strain of Priscilla growing in her womb, she placed a hand delicately on Dad's shoulder. She knew that she was the reason Dad was worried about starting the journey. He feared it would be too much for her. Mom placed his face in her hands and told him softly that God would give her the strength she needed. She was not going to sit around and risk watching her children die in her arms.

So, Dad finally decided, we were to leave in the morning. There was nothing to eat for dinner since we had eaten everything that had not already been packed. I laid on my bed, my brothers again beside me, sleep rushing over them like a flood. Afraid of what the night may bring, I fought the sleep, just like the night before. But exhaustion wrapped a warm blanket around me and the sound of gunshots slowly faded as I drifted into the dark.

Chapter Three

Through the Jungle
1996

There was commotion outside. I jumped out of bed, startled by the noise, surprised to see sunlight pouring in through the shutters. *How had I slept so long?* It seemed as if I had just closed my eyes. With a clear head and renewed strength, I bounced through the doorway and into the living room.

Inside, Dad's brother, my Uncle Ndeko, cradled a tiny baby in his arms—my cousin Christiane, only a month old. I looked out the front door and saw a caravan of about forty family members and a few of their friends. The grown-ups were carrying packs over their shoulders or large sacks on their heads. Young cousins hung on others' backs or gripped their hands. Everyone was ready to go.

After a few minutes, Mom handed me a book bag with some food and a change of clothes. I put it on backward, hanging off my shoulders down my chest. I took Christian's hand and followed my parents out the door.

Dad locked up our house and we all started walking—away from the neighborhood, away from our home, away from what, up until that point, had been our entire lives. Mom balanced a basket of food on her head while carrying Adili on her back and Priscilla in her womb. I'm still amazed by how she did that.

The rest of our supplies were wrapped in a white bed sheet, which Dad carried on his head. He was all covered up; I couldn't see his face. The pack ballooned around him, sagging over Dad's forehead just above his eyes. I choked back my laughter at the sight of him. It was like a melted marshmallow stuck to his back. I may have cracked a smile every now and then when I looked over at him, but I still appreciated that he carried the heaviest stuff so that we didn't have to.

We kept a steady pace as we marched through my neighborhood. It was creepy, like a graveyard. Everyone was gone. Bone-white stone houses stuck up out of the earth like skeletons. Crooked boards covered windows, tacked up in a hurry. I felt as if we were being watched through the hollow structures.

I was relieved when the road widened where we used to follow it to the marketplace. But I was just as quickly overwhelmed by the crowds that packed the street. The people were like ants crawling all over each other. Everyone appeared to be going a different way. It was chaos. I gripped Christian's hand tighter as bodies pushed past us—from behind, from the side, coming toward us. The masses towered over us, so my eyes glued to Dad's familiar frame, sagging under the weight of his bundle. I was afraid I might lose my parents in the rushing stream of people. But

Mom and Dad never let us stray far. Whenever John or Baraka began to lag behind, they swooped back, pushing my siblings on like newborn antelope learning to run minutes after birth. I felt them watching over me, even when their eyes were fixed on the road ahead.

As my bare feet carried me, one step at a time, my eyes and ears absorbed horrors I'll never forget. Limp bodies, painted with dry blood, were laid out on the side of the road. Women's screams, muffled by rows of vacant houses, turned my stomach even though I was too young to fully understand what was happening to them. Fresh blood poured from a man's leg as he cried out in pain. I saw the dark circle where the bullet tore through his flesh. The wounded would lay in the road, just off to the side, teeth clenched in agony, pressing hands against their bodies as dark red syrup oozed through their fingers. It pained me to watch; my chest would tense up, heart burning within, but I couldn't look away.

High-pitched wails pierced the air. Children were looking for their parents, tears streaming down their faces. Some scrambled through the sea of bodies, frantically searching for a familiar face. Other kids just sobbed in the middle of the street, scared and helpless. In the doorways of lifeless homes, frantic children yelled, "Mama! Mama!" into the crowd. No one came. They were lost in the shuffle.

I watched Christian struggling to keep up on short legs. Fighting back tears, I scooped him up and slung him across my back, locking his legs under my arms. Children no bigger than him, some even smaller, had been abandoned by their families. They were left behind to fend for themselves. Sometimes, when I close my eyes, I still see their faces—eyes barely open, pouring tears as their straining voices faded behind me.

Through the madness, Dad warned us, over and over, "Don't look back." That message would come to define my life for the coming years. *Don't look back.* Straining to keep our supplies balanced, Dad would raise the pack with the back of his hand just enough so that he could look right at my brothers and me. His dark eyes were like stones—

hard, unmoving. "Don't look behind you. Just keep moving forward, no matter what you see." The tragedy around us affected his heart, too. I could hear it in his voice, the way he carefully pronounced each syllable—thoughtful, intense. He was afraid we'd become separated, and he was determined to stay strong for us. "Stay close to the family and don't fall behind," he would repeat himself, the words churning in steady motion, driving us forward and away from the danger.

Two hours later, we followed the stream of people out of Bukavu. We only stopped to splash water into our mouths. I chewed on some sugarcane Dad had purchased from a roadside merchant. The juice was sweet in my mouth as the tough fibers ground between my teeth.

Outside the city, people marched down the dark brown road in a more orderly manner than they had in the city. Slumping under their belongings, slung over shoulders or riding atop heads, the masses filed from the city into the thick jungle. One foot in front of the other, we all walked, Bukavu disappearing behind us. The line stretched as far as I could see ahead or behind me. We were like the Israelites fleeing Egypt. I just hoped there was no vengeful army chasing after us.

Baraka cried. He did not want to walk anymore. He started dragging his feet, slowing us down. Dad was being swallowed up by our supplies. Adili's limbs were fastened tight around Mom, right above her baby bump. I was going back and forth between carrying Christian until my arms burned and then pulling him along until he gave up walking again. We had no arms to spare. Dad found a young woman who only had a small bag on her back and paid her to carry Baraka for a couple hours.

Tanks would roll by, pressing the caravan to one side, their long, heavy noses aimed at Bukavu. My heart stopped each time the massive treads chewed through the moist dirt beside me.

The regular bursts of gunfire faded as we moved into the ocean of green. Sometimes, the dying roar of an explosion or cannon fire would ripple overhead.

I'd never been this far outside of the city before, so I craned my neck, eyes wide as I looked up into the jungle canopy. Trees poked the sky, branches intertwined.

The land became steeper the further we got from the city. Over the next three hours, the crowds trickled away, taking their own paths to escape, until it was just our group. By then the trees that surrounded us towered high above us and thick underbrush tangled across the Congolese jungle floor. Mosquitos buzzed in my ears. Swatting did nothing to thin the swarms biting at my neck.

The men hacked a path through the dense forest, just enough for us to slip through. Broken sticks scraped my arms and legs; leaves bigger than my face slapped my body.

I had to watch my steps, mindful of venomous snakes hiding among the twigs and plants. People talk about big snakes, but it's the little ones you need to watch out for. It was hard to see where my feet would land, though. I was up to my waist in plants. I had grown used to running around barefoot, but the road through the jungle was brutal. Jagged rocks scraped my soles. I stumbled along, tripping on vines. The uneven ground rolled my ankles.

The road wound steeply through the forest. Sharp curves threatened to swallow us back down the mountain if we got too close to the edge. Going down, I had to be careful to lean back so that I didn't tumble into the unforgiving underbrush.

The air was heavy and moist. It was like walking through a cloud with wisps of light fog circling around us. Rain started and stopped constantly, soaking my clothes. I shivered as we pressed on, wishing for a fire to sit around and warm myself.

We walked all day. As the sun disappeared behind the mountains, we arrived at a small village—Ngueshe, just a few huts poking out of the trees. I heard the men questioning whether it was safe for us to stop, but at that point, we had no other option. Mom was breathing in deep, exhaling slowly, pressing out her belly even further as she stretched her back.

A small, frail woman, hair hidden beneath a rainbow wrap, came out of a modest grass hut to greet us. She took care of six grandchildren. The woman's kind eyes, buried by wrinkles, emerged as she invited us to eat.

Me and the other boys attacked the trees—guava juice running down our chins as we stuffed bananas and avocados into our mouths. I ate so fast I almost choked myself. The women from our group helped our hostess wrap cornmeal—which we called *fufu*—in cassava leaves. We ate the wraps raw even though there was a risk of poisoning from eating uncooked cassava. But we didn't care; all of us were so hungry. We drank right from the stream, too. The bacteria-infested water was cool and refreshing as we gulped it down, cupping handful after handful to our mouths.

When it was time for bed, the girls and women crammed into a hut, laying body to body, while the boys and men stayed outside. In the waist-high grass, I found a *rungu*—a long, heavy club, straight with a thick knot on one end. The jungle ceiling blotted out the night sky; only patches of stars poked through. I gripped the club until my hands were numb. I didn't know what lurked beneath the inky blanket of shadows. Outlines of trunks and branches in the night were like the open jaws of wild animals, hungry. Even with my brothers on either side of me and twenty of my cousins watching out for leopards, gorillas, or human attackers, I was still afraid. I feared that bad men would appear from the dense fortress and kill us all in the night. *If we die out here, no one would ever know.*

For the second time in three days, I couldn't close my eyes all night. My heartbeat drummed in my ears as I clutched my club, fighting to quiet my rapid breathing. Heavy leaves would fall, crashing through the brush, triggering a rush through my body. To pass the time, we told stories. The darkness disappeared behind pictures in my head—dramatic soccer games, enchanting girls—as our voices painted the night.

We ended up spending two nights in Ngueshe. The next day, Dad and Uncle Ndeko heard news of attacks in the region ahead. We made a small fire outside for the second night; we risked signaling our position to rebels, but it was a welcome gamble. The glowing embers warmed my body and melted my fears. I slept soundly on the damp ground, amber light flickering across my face, the rungu hugged to my chest.

It was an early start, following the sun upward as we marched toward the top of the next mountain. Then down into another lush valley. Then up again. The vines and sticks and thorns punished me the entire way. Christian weighed heavy on my back—I thought he must've had more than his share from those fruit trees. We walked until my feet were raw, crying for relief. But we kept moving, one look at Mom reminded us all that no matter how bad we thought it was, it could be worse.

We trudged up Eastern Congolese mountains and cut through valleys until close to midnight. Exhaustion weighed on me—I felt as if we were climbing up to the moon. Just as I thought my legs were going to give out under me, we arrived at a plateau. Over the steep incline, the land stretched wide before us. The trees were not so numerous or thick. The silver moonlight revealed five or six houses dotting the landscape.

The warm glow of lamps drew us closer. I could smell meat sizzling over open fires—there were people waiting up for us. They had slaughtered four goats and prepared rice and green beans. My mouth watered, and I forgot how tired I was.

Grandpa Ntibonera came running out to greet us from his wide, brick house. We had never met him before—the journey was not practical for my parents with so many small children. There was a party of at least thirty-five family members and friends waiting to celebrate our arrival. The others crowded around us as Grandpa pulled me in tight, his beard rough against my cheek.

Tears streamed down my face—all of us were crying, a shower of emotion born out of relief. There was so much joy in seeing all of the friendly faces that greeted us. We were also broken with sorrow knowing that so many other families did not make it on their escape journeys. It was only by God's hand that we had been spared, and so we were grateful.

The party lasted for two hours before my muscles called for the same relief that I felt inside at having finished the difficult journey. Everyone else must have felt the same way because the commotion faded as quickly as it had begun. I collapsed in a bed of soft grass. There was nothing to fear now, it seemed, and I fell asleep as quickly as I shut my eyes. I felt hope—hope that my motherland would return to peace, that life could return to normal.

Chapter Four

Banana Sledding in Kaziba
1996-1997

We had to get up early. Before the sun rose, the mountains in the distance were painted in shades of blue—the ones closest were navy, almost black, and they got lighter as you looked further, melting purple into the orange sky. This was not the city anymore. My eyes would have rather missed the beauty before them, though, to be closed for another hour.

With an axe leaned against my shoulder and a machete flapping at my side, I made my way to the fields for work.

Grandpa Ntibonera's village, Kaziba, was nestled in the mountains of the Eastern Congo on a rolling, green stretch of land. For me, it was a new world. And it took time adapting to my new life.

When I first arrived in the village, I was sick for three days. Drinking water from the wild streams soured my stomach. It flushed out of my system from both ends. My body was so weak I could hardly move, and I burned with fever. When I wasn't doubled over, throwing up, I would lie on the floor of my grass hut—it was round with a tall, pointed roof—sweating and shaking on the soft, yellow grass. I shared the hut with my brothers and about ten of my cousins. Most of them, including all of my brothers, experienced these symptoms those first few days.

From then on, we boiled all of our drinking water in pots over the fire.

The soil was contaminated with parasites—jiggers, which burrowed into the skin and fed on the flesh. In Kaziba, I ran and played without shoes, just like I always had. I didn't have a pair of shoes, and the sandals I was supposed to wear (but never did) were somewhere on the floor of our home in Bukavu. Jiggers are nasty little bugs, like fleas, that dig into your toes or fingers—anywhere they can get in, really—and begin to lay eggs, devouring and rotting the soft tissue as they multiply. The infections were rampant across the village—wounds black and swollen, like burns. Children with hands and feet rotting to soggy, fleshy stumps. At that point, the only solution is amputation.

More than once, I contracted the parasites. It was unbearably itchy at first, and then my skin would burn in pain. My body would catch fire, sweating and vomiting from the fever. We had no medicine to ease the symptoms, we just had to dig them out and let the sickness pass. All I wanted to do was scratch and pick at them, but that would only make the sores flare up.

The worst time was when the jiggers chewed into my knee. First my skin bubbled white, then it started to char a smoky black. Larvae writhed in the tunnels in my skin. The pain funneled downward, causing the joint to ache. My forehead felt cold and wet even though it was hot to the touch.

To get them out, we had to use needles. I'd grit my teeth as Mom poked the sharp point into my wounds, the cool metal stinging as she scraped. White slime oozed from the tiny holes. John and Baraka also suffered from jiggers. We helped each other fish them out, fraying skin with the needlepoint, lancing the parasites out. As time went on, we were more careful to spot signs of jiggers early and clean out the sites before they got so bad that they started to swell.

For an entire year, I did not go to school. But that didn't mean that I got to run around and play or throw concerts all day. My new classroom was the unforgiving land, which I had to work for hours each day in the blazing sun.

Grandpa owned several acres and provided my family with about five acres of rugged, overgrown land to farm. My parents lived in a room in his house, where some other aunts and uncles also stayed. There were a few smaller houses and huts fanned out across his property. Like us boys, the girl cousins also shared a hut.

It took a month of preparation to get the land ready to plant.

My hands blistered as I swung the axe, chopping down trees. It never rained. The sun always seemed to be hot and heavy overhead. After eight to ten hours slashing through thick bushes and grass with the machete, my arms felt like rubber. I had to turn up the soil to get it ready to plant, rocks and roots fighting the hoe as it bit into the ground. I would have to weed by hand, clawing away earth, dirt caked under my fingernails, thorns scraping my skin.

My parents did a lot of the hard work, digging up and hauling away heavy rocks. Mom was out there even when Priscilla pushed against her belly, ready to come out.

The field was planted with cassava. We ground up the long, brown tubers with green plantain flour to make fufu, a main part of our diet.

Mom and Dad prayed together in the field before it was time to collect our first harvest. Rows of hand-shaped leaves waved their bright green fingers as my parents pulled up the plump stalks from the soil. God blessed the land incredibly. Grandpa could not believe that the tough land could produce so much.

The first thing Dad did was give his first fruits back to the Lord. We carried baskets overflowing with food, my arms straining under their weight, to the village church. The offering was used to feed needy families in the area. There was more than enough cassava leftover to feed our family, for us to share anytime we knew somebody needed a meal, and even for Dad to sell. Witnessing how Dad gave his very best to the Lord showed me how God can use us to bless others. By following Abel's biblical example of offering your best rewards to God—who provided it in the first place—Dad demonstrated how to properly order our lives. By trusting God, we were able to be generous to others and still receive what we needed. We never went hungry while we were in the village.

God also blessed our family with another baby girl. After carrying her across the mountains, through thick jungles, and while straining to turn up dirt under the burning sun, Mom delivered Priscilla in Grandpa Ntibonera's house. Grandma Ntibonera gathered my aunts to help with the home birth. My brothers and I were told to stay outside, but we clearly heard the sound of Priscilla's breathy wails tell us that she was OK.

Baby Priscilla brought so much joy to our lives in the midst of a difficult transition. We'd watch her soft face rest peacefully against Mom's chest as she rocked the baby by the fire. Priscilla reminded us that life kept moving on, that God never stopped working.

Once my parents got the field running, I got to help my cousins and uncles with the livestock. We led the animals to patchy, open fields, littered with bushes, to graze and then took them down to the river for water. The village was surrounded by dark, unforgiving jungle so we had to be on our toes at all times with the cows and goats. If you took your eyes away for a second, they would scatter in different directions and then we would have to spend all afternoon chasing after them, driving them back to the barn. I kept a homemade bow slung across my chest, like my cousins did. The older boys taught me how to use it. While keeping a watchful eye on the flocks, we would scan the field for rabbits. It was good fun trying to hit one with an arrow—hunting helped pass the time and, if successful, gave us a good meal later. The meat would slide right off the bone as I bit in, nice and tender.

Grandpa Ntibonera also kept a pen of rabbits near the house. One time, I discovered a trail of fur and streaks of fresh blood. A fox or jungle cat had stolen an easy meal in the night. Though I played the brave shepherd boy during the day—imagining I was like David in the Bible, ready to fight panthers instead of lions—at night I was terrified of what crept in the dark. There were only a few generators in the village, which were hardly ever used, and each night the kerosene lamps drifted off to sleep, one-by-one. Only a faint silver glow held back the wild, black unknown.

On nights when I couldn't sleep, I'd peek out of the hut, and tree branches would transform into lean, muscled limbs, stalking me—catlike, wooden claws extended. After seeing what was left of Grandpa's rabbits, I wouldn't even go out at night to relieve myself.

Life in the village was simple and traditional. People did not talk much, but they were friendly. Everyone was focused on working hard to keep their own plots of land producing.

Sundays were different. It was like the people cracked through their dirt-crusted shells when they crammed into the long, brick church building. The whole village attended. For hours our bodies would bake inside, sweat glistening our foreheads. We belted *nyimbo za wokovu* between roaring sermons, thumping the bare ground, drumming the wooden benches, and beating our hands together. Sometimes, the pastor let Dad preach. Veins popped out of his neck as his voice rumbled off the hard walls and he shook his finger toward Heaven. With the congregation on their feet, hands raised and eyes closed, echoing each others' "amens," Dad would drop his voice, just loud enough for the people in the back to hear. You could catch your breath. But the gentle words rustled the chambers of your heart. Then, Dad would drive home his point with thunder, stirring a movement of the spirit in the room. I've always loved listening to my father preach.

Even though there was not a lot to do in the village, I didn't have much time to complain. All the boys would play soccer. Just like in the city, before my friends and I were able to get equipment, we balled up plastic trash bags, wrestling them away from each other with our feet, kicking them between sticks we stabbed into the ground.

We could play soccer anywhere, anytime, all day long. But the village also brought new adventures. Together, us boys would climb up into the mountains, chop down banana trees, and carve the trunks into sleds. We'd find a steep hill, grass slick with dew, and ride our sleds down the slope. We fit two or three at a time, single file. I could feel the ground knocking against the sled, bumping me along, as I raced to the bottom. It was such a thrill—wind rushing past my ears, my heart pounding within me before I wiped out on the dirt. That is if I was lucky. If you went too fast the sled would crash into a sharp, tangled knot of a bush. I went home with my share of warm, wet gashes and deep splinters. Our parents did not appreciate the sledding very much.

All the boys enjoyed riding the banana sleds down the hill. Christian, however, loved it most of all. He was just a toddler—two, three years old—but we could never leave him behind to go sledding. If he found out we flew downhill without him, he would pierce our ears with his cries. Christian would scurry to the top and wedge himself between whoever was about to go down next; it was always his turn, according to Christian. He screamed with joy the whole way, his voice trailing down the slide until it stopped abruptly, the wind knocked out of Christian. Crackling giggles would erupt as he picked himself up and bounded back uphill.

I also enjoyed really getting to know my Grandpa Ntibonera. He was a quiet, thoughtful man. After a day of hard work, he would sit in front of the fire, absorbing the flames with his deep eyes as all of us grandchildren sat around him. Adili or one of the other little ones would climb up into his lap and play with his full, gray beard while he told us stories. Another little one would jump up onto his long back, but he didn't mind. He would tell us about the lion chasing after the antelope through the savannah, patiently answering every interrupting question. We loved those stories—our eyes would grow wide as he took us through every turn and leap of the hunt.

Grandpa would call me from my hut to help him feed the pigs, swallowing back the last of his strong, dark coffee. He never went a day without his coffee. I was always looking up to him, and not just because he was so tall. Everyone in the community admired him: he was highly respected, known for his generosity.

After a year in Kaziba, Dad visited Bukavu and decided that it was safe enough to go home. He took my brothers and I ahead, planning to come back for the girls.

Christian kept up much better now that his legs had grown much longer and a bit stronger. The journey through the jungle seemed to pass much quicker this time. I felt like we had something to look forward to, not to run from. But I was reminded that this was not the same Congo that I was born into.

Along the way, we came to a busy hub where people were selling goods to travelers. There were tracks in the dirt from where buses stopped as they passed through. Dad was a few paces ahead, stepping purposefully like a man who knew where he was headed. Without realizing it, Dad walked right up to a wooden barrier. As Dad passed by, about six or seven men raised rifles and started yelling at him in Swahili.

They shouted: *"Wewe!" "Wewe!"*—"You!" "You," trying to get his attention.

Dad went pale.

I was only about ten feet back. Quickly, I pulled my brothers close, squeezing all three of them tightly against me.

The men were all mismatched, in street clothes. I saw a few more appear from an old building behind the barrier, heavy boots packing the dirt beneath them. They trained their guns on Dad.

People stopped what they were doing to see what was going on. They stared like a herd of cows made suddenly aware of a predator approaching. My brothers and I watched in horror—there was nothing we could do. My face flushed, hot as the sun. Holding my brothers together, our arms tangled around each other, I fumbled out some words resembling a prayer.

The men kept shouting. They were wondering why Dad dared to pass by their barrier. Other men had been beaten and shot for doing such a thing. The dark stains in the earth around them proved that they were not messing around.

With the butt of a gun, Dad was forced to his knees. He held his tongue and kept his hands raised. The men taunted my dad. They kicked dirt at him, snarled, like jackals, as he just took their insults, frozen.

All I wanted to do was run to him. My muscles tensed, ready to spring toward him. But as I was about to take off, I caught an old man's eye. Without a word, his milky, heavy eyes warned me not to move. It would be worse for everyone.

Minutes ticked by. Each second my heart raced a little harder. My mouth dried up. I kept whispering broken prayers in my brothers' ears.

Dad knew that if he said the wrong thing, made any sort of smart comment, then his life would be over. The men kept their barrels trained on him as they continued making a scene. They'd press their guns up against the back of his head like they were going to execute him. I just held my breath. None of us could cry, not even little Christian. We were statues. Terrified statues.

Just as I thought that my fear was going to crack my ribs and burst out of me, one of the men gave Dad a sharp, strong kick from behind. "Get out of here!" he yelled as Dad sprinted over to us. Everyone around us got back to what they were doing, nervously keeping their distance from the barrier, where the men acted as if nothing happened. They blew cigarette smoke from their mouths and noses, rifles resting on their shoulders.

The tears came then as Dad, relatively unharmed, wrapped his strong arms around us and thanked the Lord for his protection. I was shaking, overwhelmed. I had just witnessed a miracle.

Chapter Five

City in Chaos
1997-2000

A rriving in our familiar marketplace, my roadside stage was quiet, vacant, patches of grass creeping up through the dirt. Now, rather than music, an eerie murmur hummed through the streets as people went about their business.

Dust swirled in the air around Dad's shop—he rented a convenience store-sized building at the market where he sold dry goods in large quantities. The windows were clouded by the year gone by. The glass was almost as white as the stone walls they were set in. The wooden door leaned lazily against its hinges, cracked. Someone had kicked it in. Inside was a mess. Shelves were toppled over, leaning at unstable angles on top of one another. Grains of sugar dusted the floorboards. Some dry beans and rice scattered around. There was nothing left.

Looters had established a new order in Bukavu—rather than working for what you had, people just took what they wanted if they were strong and ruthless enough.

Disappointment sagged on Dad's face. Though his business had been ransacked, he didn't fret. Dad let out a slow breath and turned to me and my brothers, patting my shoulder lightly. "Thank God we are alive," he said. Then, he fished a broom out of the debris, leaned it against the wall, and began setting the shelves upright. My brothers and I joined in without saying a word.

Remarkably, our house was untouched. Destruction surrounded our neighborhood—windows had been shattered, doors were fractured, and hurried tracks, in and out, were carved in the dirt. Somehow our compound had been overlooked. We praised God for wrapping His arms around our neighborhood.

After settling in for a week-and-a-half, Dad went back to Kaziba to bring Mom and the girls home. I felt relieved to have all of us under one roof again. I was ready to put the fear of the past year out of mind and move on. But the nightmare had just begun.

Many people know about the 1994 Rwandan Genocide, when eight hundred thousand people were murdered in about one hundred days[7], all in a sick ethnic cleansing effort. As Rwanda stabilized in the wake of this, approximately two million people flooded into the Congo as refugees[8]. Some of the men who fled through Congo's Eastern border—which is relatively unsecure and easy to pass through—were hiding because they had been part of the violent uprising. The refugee camps were used by these bad men to recruit followers and terrorize the local population. They started to organize militia—many were already active in the area (like the one that attacked my dad)—seeking to control the minerals my motherland was supplying to the modern world.

The First Congo War ignited as East Congolese militarized to force the rebels out of the country. But Rwanda and Uganda sent armies in support of the rebels, occupying Eastern Congo and eventually overthrowing Mobutu II's regime. Hundreds of thousands died[9]. My motherland's name was changed from Zaire to the Democratic Republic of the Congo and Laurent-Désiré Kabila took over as the new president.

The violence lessened for a brief period between the First Congo War, the one that forced my family from our home in 1996, and the Second Congo War. This gave us an illusion of safety, believing that we could come home and rebuild our lives.

But there was never any real peace between the first and second wars. The Eastern Congo remained a war zone, unstable with chaos reigning. Kabila soon angered his Ugandan and Rwandan supporters, setting off what would become the Second Congo War in 1998.

This is all history, but at the time, for me and my family, it was reality; we were living it. I didn't understand what was going on politically. I just knew my motherland was unraveling before my eyes.

When we returned to Bukavu, people were different. It was like the fear in the air was weighing down on them as they walked—shoulders tense, faces drawn tight. Their eyes shifted nervously. People were more guarded, too. When they exchanged money and goods, they were quick about it, watching the other carefully. No wasted words. The common trust among the people had been stolen by looters as well.

Walking down the street, you'd see curtains ruffle, eyes watching. One day I would pass a shop, the owner quiet and cautious as he tried to make his living. The next time I would walk by, there would be no one there—just broken wood and flat boxes scarred by boot treads.

I knew so many families who lost everything. They returned to the neighborhood with sunken eyes, bodies worn to the bone from hunger. Before the war, they had lived good lives. But their businesses had been stormed, everything of value taken. To survive, they just waited and scavenged, living like birds. These people would wander the streets, offering work in exchange for a meal.

For days, sometimes a couple weeks at a time, the city around us would settle, like still water. But an eerie feeling hung in the air—the surface, we knew, would ripple at any moment. I felt it in my chest as I watched people stiffening up as they passed. My heart beat faster as I rounded every street corner, each alley. Then, one day, the gunfire would crash overhead, like a storm. People would lock themselves inside and wait for the downpour to stop. After a few days, it was back to the quiet tension, anticipating another eruption. For an eight-year-old like myself, it was hard to just be a kid.

At first, I would go to school during the calm periods. I could not focus in the classroom. My blue-and-white uniform felt like it was choking me as I fidgeted my feet under my desk, tapping my pencil nervously against the wood. My eyes would float out the window, drifting across the blue emptiness while my ears searched for warning signs.

There were always whispers that bad men were coming. Eventually, the rumors would spread across my school like wildfire, and everyone would run home. The teachers couldn't stop it.

When the guns were screaming, we didn't go to school. At least on those days I could feel the weight of our brick walls around me at home. I knew Mom and Dad would be there if anything happened. When the city was still, and we tried to act like everything was normal, it felt like you were standing on glass about to shatter.

One day it did. It had just rained, and the air was still heavy. Students flashed in a blur past the doorway to my classroom, one after another. I slipped into the hall and asked two kids—a brother and sister—what was going on as they hurried by. "The rebels are coming," the brother called over his shoulder, dragging his sister along.

Boys and girls started rushing out of the classrooms. I stumbled forward, bumped from behind as students pushed by. The rumor fire had caught. I ran back inside and grabbed my backpack. I took off, slinging the strap over my shoulder, not bothering to turn back for the books I'd left on my desk. By the time I reached the courtyard, there were already a couple hundred kids funneling out the gate, only wide enough for two or three at a time. People started panicking. Bodies piled up, pushing each other toward the iron bars, fighting to get to the opening. Kids slipped, crashing into the mud, feet trampling over them. Smaller children cried as bigger ones nearly crushed them.

The school drained, the rest of the five hundred or so students crashing into us from behind. I kept leaning forward, weaving through the mass. I didn't bother looking back since I knew that all of my siblings had stayed home that day. A distant rattle of gunfire slipped into my ears, almost completely drowned by the moist pops of feet tearing through mud. Squeezed from every side, I thought I might burst. I pressed with all my might to the exit, heart in my throat. I fought to breathe.

Finally, I fell through the opening, landing on my palms in the slick mud. Kids continued to spill out of the iron gate, knocking my shoulders as they ran past me. I didn't wait to catch my breath. I just wiped my hands on my thighs and started running, the houses blurring together, forming a tunnel on either side as I raced home, spraying wet earth with each stride.

Three days later, I was back in school again, the city balanced on a fresh sheet of glass.

Mom hardly left the house. She did her best to keep Adili and Priscilla, who were now wobbling around the house on unsteady feet, out of sight, too. And I saw the way Mom watched over Asi, and then Naomi, as well, after they were born—a year apart while we were back living in Bukavu. When she rocked my sisters, Mom whispered prayers over their little heads. Mom prayed for each of us kids, all the time.

When we were babies, she would rest her hand on our backs while we slept. Out loud, in a voice so sweet it almost sounded like singing, Mom would ask God that we would grow up to love the Lord and serve Him in whatever we did. While we were living in the unstable Bukavu that we had returned to, those prayers seemed more urgent. There was an edge in her melodic voice, even if you couldn't detect it with your ears.

Though my parents did their best to shelter me and my brothers, we understood enough—Bukavu was not a safe place for girls. Unspeakable horrors were taking place all over the city. We did not know who the bad men were or why they were doing this. We just knew they were forcing themselves inside people's houses. It was happening all around us. We were just children, living with the very real fear that the bad men would come to our house and do terrible things, or make us do those horrible things, and then take us away to force us to become one of them.

I felt powerless. I was getting taller, but not much heavier—meals weren't as plentiful as before. I did not understand why these awful things were happening to my people. I felt bad because I knew evil was happening, ruining my city, and I did not think there was anything that I could do to stop it. In the night, John and I would wrestle our fears together. It was hard to sleep. Whispering through the dark, arms wrapped in our sheets, we prepared ourselves for when the rebels came.

"We can't let anything happen to our family," I would say, tensing up. "I'd rather die fighting than let the men come in and harm us."

"We'll fight, together," John offered.

It helped me fall asleep—and John would say the same, knowing we had each other's backs. Talking out loud eased the worry. Even if we were planning for the worst. Some nights, as me and John pledged to fight to the death for our family, Baraka—lying still, pretending to sleep, listening—would cut in, "Me, too." We were just kids. But together we felt stronger.

As we slept, and even in daylight, rebels were going door-to-door, insisting to be let in, breaking down doors if they were not. The bad men stole anything of value they could find. They raped girls, as young as ten years old. These evil men would force themselves into a home, they would come in and they would rape your mom or your sister, right in front of the men and boys. They might take one of the boys and make him rape his own mother or sister. It was a plague, an evil sickness, spreading in my motherland.

For the rebels, rape was a weapon to exert power, to destroy communities and tear families apart. It was about instilling fear in the people. Then, they would use that fear to control them.

Unfortunately, rape was successful in destroying communities. Rape caused marriages to fall apart; men would leave their wives, as if they had anything to do with what happened. Neighbors shunned girls from the community if it was discovered they had been raped. Children of rape were abandoned, kicked out of their own homes, and forced to fend for themselves.

Victims did not know who to turn to or whom they could trust. Some girls would report the abuse to the authorities—looking for help from those who were supposed to protect them—and get no help. Some of those men in power were guilty of rape themselves. These women, and girls, believed they could not tell anyone. They were afraid of being kicked out of their families. So many victims suffered in silence. The rapists, however, marched through the streets, announcing themselves with earth-quaking steps.

I remember the sound—a loud thud exploded, right across the street, in broad daylight. The sun was still climbing toward midday. I turned to see a tall man, wearing a green jacket and thick, black boots, kicking against my neighbor's door. He carried a big gun. It looked heavy. Down the street I noticed more green jackets approaching. Rebels were going door-to-door, robbing homes one after the other.

I could just pick up slaps and dull thumps, falling like rain in the distance. They were beating anyone who resisted. And worse. I didn't hear the screams, but later I saw the tear-stained faces of women, hollow, drained of emotion.

With the tall man's back still to me, I threw myself inside the house. My body forced the door closed as the realization slammed me against it. *We were next.*

I warned my family, fighting not to scream. I ducked under the window with my brothers to try and watch what was happening.

Every time I peeked outside, I couldn't see anything, and I was too afraid to keep my head up for too long. I heard banging and crashing, like things being broken, thrown across a room. I wondered what the bad men were looking for.

Dad, gripping the polished leather of his Bible, signaled for us to gather around him in the living room. We circled tight on the floor. Our heads nearly touched as we prayed for protection. The words on the page barely reached my ears as Dad recited scriptures. But they filled the room with power. "The Lord is my rock, my fortress, and my savior," he read. "My God is my rock, in whom I find protection. He is my shield, the power that saves me, and my place of safety" (Psalm 18:2, NLT). I looked up to my Dad in that moment, and through him I saw God's strength.

After five minutes, commotion still alive across the street, Dad told us to go back into hiding. The girls scurried to the room all the way at the back. With Naomi rocking in her arms, Mom went from room-to-room, praying for the blood of Jesus to cover our house.

I crouched next to my brothers. Their warmth reminded me that I wasn't alone, that we were still alive, as we waited. The fear gripped my whole body—I felt like I couldn't move as the seconds ticked by.

Maybe half an hour, maybe more passed by before I heard the rebels' voices in the open air. The hand of fear melted away as a new sensation washed over me. My ears were hot, pulse racing. I was so afraid, but my body was no longer frozen—it was wound tight, like a string about to snap. Boot steps started thumping, louder and louder, my heart following the rhythm. The light creeping through the shutters darkened. I looked at John. Our gazes locked. *This is it*, our eyes said. *Do or die.*

The men planted their feet outside the door. I tensed up; bracing myself for the crash I knew was coming.

But it never did. Instead, I heard a distant voice, sharp and direct, followed by mumbled groans outside our house. I was too shocked to understand what they were saying, but I realized as the voices trailed off that the men had been called back by their commander. They started complaining because they wanted to finish what they had started, but they wouldn't dare defy an order.

I don't know how long I waited, convinced the men would come back. I couldn't believe it. When I set my breath free, relief started to fill my lungs. The air around me was lighter, even though me and my brothers had not yet loosened our grips on each other. My legs finally found the strength to lift me off the ground, and I ran to where Mom and Dad had the girls locked up in a hug, fitting myself securely in the embrace.

We stayed together, all day and into the night, hardly able to speak, praising God with whatever words we could manage.

Less than two weeks later, Dad sold everything we had: our house, his business—everything except what we needed to wear. He decided we needed to leave the Congo. God had delivered us, but Dad saw that as a warning that it was no longer safe for us there. He was not going to stay and witness his wife being abused, his children murdered. We had to leave the fear behind.

After the rebels had come to our door, Dad was lost. He wrestled with the weight of his decision. Mom approached him three days later and told him that God had sent her a vision in a dream—she saw our family fleeing the country. Dad took this very seriously and disappeared for a week, praying and fasting, only having water to drink.

Dad decided to go to Kenya, alone, and declare himself a refugee. He would settle there and come for us once he knew that he could arrange safe passage for all of us, together. The reason he went ahead was because it would be much more difficult for our entire family to be granted asylum. Dad knew that if could get established, it would make the process faster for the rest of us.

People thought he had gone crazy. Relatives kept insisting that it was better to die in your own country than to live in another land. Dad would tell them he was taking a step of faith, trusting in God. "I am not going to watch my family get killed," he would say.

Early on a Thursday morning, the whole family accompanied Dad to the Rwandan border. He had a suitcase in each hand. Mom kept her head up, her eyes dry. She believed in Dad and wanted us to as well. Dad set the luggage down and started hugging us one-by-one. First, he hugged the boys, John, Baraka, and Christian, and then the older girls—Adili, Priscilla, and Asi.

After saying goodbye to my siblings, Dad pulled me tight. I felt how heavy his heart was as it beat against mine. When his arms loosened their grip, Dad looked me in the eye, and spoke: "We will meet again," he said, loud enough for the whole family to hear. "I promise I will come for you."

Then he told me that while he was gone, I was the man of our house.

Dad then hugged Naomi, but she didn't want to let him go. She started crying, arms locked around his neck, causing everyone else to start crying, too. Except Mom. She did not shed any tears as she pried Naomi loose. Mom gently reassured us that everything would be fine. We would see him soon. Mom hugged Dad tight and kissed him goodbye before we watched him disappear over the border. Then, I felt all of their eyes on me.

Chapter Six

Internally Displaced
2000-2002

I thought my back was going to snap in two. The sun had been beating me all day as I carried load after load of bricks on my head up a steady incline to where the construction workers were pasting them together in rows. My arms felt like they were going to fall off when I dropped the burden on the dry ground and ran the back of my hand across my forehead, slick as a leaf in the misty jungle. John exhaled hard beside me.

Evening was beginning to creep up over the city as we headed back to the field to retrieve our last load. My neck was stiff but walking downhill with empty hands was a relief. John and I had been at work since just after dawn, and, after two weeks of trudging uphill, bending under the weight of the bricks only to be sent back down for another load with words like whips, I was ready to collapse. The other workers drove us hard, yelling at John and I for not going faster even though we wore our bodies to exhaustion. It was a twenty-minute climb up that hill. We worked every couple of days, when a massive truck rolled into an empty field at the bottom of the hill and dumped a mountain of bricks on the ground. The road going up into the neighborhood where construction was taking place was too steep and narrow for the truck, so we carried the load up to the workers, piece by piece.

There was a bald patch, dry and dead, in the grass marking our progress. I didn't notice the pressure on my spine as I marched the last of the bricks to the worksite, John at my heels. My heart was beating fast, but this time it was in anticipation—today, finally, we were going to get paid. It was the reward that had kept us going.

But when me and John raised our palms to the foreman, they were pushed away. Bending back my sore neck to look up at the man, whose head was pinched above tight shoulders, I asked again for our pay. He told me to get out of there. Now my pulse was racing, my ears hot, even though the air temperature was crawling down for the day. I stamped my foot. John scowled. We started to panic—all that work, for what? The man snarled, like a jackal baring yellow teeth, as he swatted a massive paw in my direction. "There is no money for you!" he barked. "Get out of here before I beat you two!" He kicked the ground by our feet, spraying dust on our legs as John and I finally ran off, afraid of what he might do.

We could not keep up the fast pace for long. We were so tired. And the disappointment of being cheated out of a week's worth of wages was heavier than anything we had lifted onto our heads. The part of town where the construction was taking place, up in the steeper, hilly parts of Bukavu, was half an hour by foot from where we were staying. So, the humiliation that me and my brother just faced bore down on us the whole way home. My neck was still stiff as I walked downhill with empty hands and empty pockets.

Mom was at the stove with Naomi scooting on the floor by her feet. Our small two-bedroom apartment felt like another blow to my stomach, on top of what had just happened. I couldn't take it anymore. I started crying. So did John. My hopes had been crushed after weeks of hard work. My efforts to try and help my family to get by had been all for nothing.

Mom came over to us and wrapped her arms around us, soft pats easing the drumming aches in our bodies and tender words soothing the burning pain in our hearts.

Before he left, Dad moved my mom, siblings, and I into the apartment so that he could sell our house to have enough money for us to start a new life outside of the Congo. He did not know where he was going, so Dad could not take us—my Mom and eight children, one still a baby and another hardly walking. His plan was to find a safe place to settle and come and get us. But Dad didn't realize how difficult it would be to reunite with us once he declared himself a refugee in Kenya—more than eight hundred miles away.

Every few months, Dad would call to check on us, telling us that he was still working to get us to him. Meanwhile, we were living as refugees within our own motherland—internally displaced persons (I.D.P.s).

There was no respect for my family in our new neighborhood. People gave us strange looks because we had such a big family, like we were somehow a burden on them. The woman who lived next door would walk right into our apartment without warning, looking for a matchbox. She owned the building, but I never once saw Dad act like that when he had tenants of his own. He treated people with dignity, and was considerate of their space, even if it was rented from him. The neighbor woman would light charcoal for her stove in a bowl right on my seat, leaving gray ash all over it and filling the room with chalky smoke. I couldn't say anything—as an eleven-year-old child it was not my place. And even though she did not act with respect, I was still expected to. My parents' lessons had taken deep roots. Plus, we needed a place to sleep.

Whenever we were invited over to the neighbor's house, she would not let us touch the furniture. She made us wait while she took the cushions off so that we could sit on the hard, bare wood. She said that we were dirty. This is the sort of treatment we received in our new community.

The violence from the war over Bukavu became a dull hum in the backs of our minds. It was almost normal. People were being slaughtered. I would hear about bodies found, blood splattered all over the bed and the walls, in the victims' own homes. But children became so used to the sounds of gunfire that they didn't take them seriously anymore. When kids heard the shots blasting in the distance, they would pretend like they were being hit, throwing their arms up, shaking around with their tongues out. They would also mimic the gun sounds by striking a certain kind of wood. When some of the neighborhood kids heard the, *Bap! Bap! Bap!*—gunshots overhead— they would play along, recreating the sounds. It was a game to them.

I stopped going to school completely after Dad left. I felt a responsibility to help take care of my family, so I started working. After the gut punch in trying to work in construction, I decided to go into business for myself. Mom let me take some of the money that we had to get us by, and I used it to buy peanuts in bulk from the marketplace and then hawk them for a profit.

I carried the nuts all day in a rectangular wooden box, calling out after businessmen as they rushed between buildings. I had to be quick on my feet, following as the crowds moved throughout the day, trying to stay in front of people so that the robust peanut scent could lure them in. Even though my business did well, it was not enough to support my family.

One day I remember walking through the door and knowing something was not right. I sensed it as I approached the apartment. When I came inside it wasn't what was there that told me what the problem was—it was what wasn't there. My mouth was dry. Normally, Mom's cooking would fill the air with some mouth-watering aroma. My stomach reminded me that it was time to eat, but Mom looked at me with sad eyes, her lips forcing a bent smile, trying to offer something that could fill me up.

Before then, hunger had always seemed like a fly, something that bothers you occasionally until you shoo it away. Now, it was an angry hornet, stinging me over and over. There was no relief. When the stinging would pass, my belly just throbbed.

All the money I made from my business went toward helping feed the family. Once my day was done, I'd press through the crowds, tightly clutching my cloth money bag as hands like vipers struck at me from all sides. Pickpockets were quick, but I was clever enough to dodge them and make it home with all my earnings. I needed every penny—there were eight of us kids, plus Mom, and what I made did not go very far. If there were any leftover peanuts, we would share them. Even if it was just a handful, I tried to make sure everyone got a bite.

John would sometimes fetch water for the neighbors in exchange for a meal. He only did this when it had been a day or two without food because they would just give him their scraps, stuff they wouldn't touch themselves. But he ate anything edible that he could get his hands on, like a scavenger. In the war-torn city, however, even something as simple as going to the well was no longer safe. When I learned this lesson, I was thankful to have been by my brother's side.

I carried the jug while John accompanied me to the well. It was dry and hot when we made the more than half-hour journey; we never seemed to need water when it was cool. When the houses around us opened up to the flat field that surrounded the well, there was already a long line. Just as I took my place behind the last person in line, I heard a familiar chorus of yelling over a rhythm of thumps and running. Soccer. I set the jug down, marking my spot, and ran off to join. John was already ahead of me.

While we were playing, a pickup truck pulled in across the field. The truck looked like it had come from the mountains; it was very dirty, mud sprayed up the sides. Out of the vehicle, I saw five men in olive green uniforms appear, carrying guns. They were smiling. The men let the kids come up to them and look at their guns. They handed out candies. Kids started running around by the truck, jumping up into the bed and back down, their bare feet stomping around the men's thick combat boots when the sweets were being offered again. Our soccer game stopped as most of the boys ran over to see what they could get.

Anytime we saw a truck going down the road in Bukavu, us kids would chase after it, legs stretching as far as they could trying to keep up. We'd run until we were left in a cloud of dust. It was fun, and sometimes you could get the driver to stop and give you a ride if you needed to get to another part of town. On this day, however, I didn't feel the normal rush of excitement pulling me toward the vehicle. My mouth didn't even water at the thought of candy. I had an uneasy feeling, like I was sick, even though my body felt fine. I watched with wary eyes from a distance.

When John's eyes started getting wider, and I noticed that he was a few steps closer than he had been before, I walked up beside him. A couple other boys had hung back as well. I heard them talking, voices low. "Don't go over there," they were saying. I remembered the rumors— kids playing in the streets and then abducted, never heard from again. The men were telling kids to get in the truck. Frantic, I yelled, "Don't go," and grabbed John by the arm. "Let's get out of here," I told him.

John didn't hesitate and started running, picking up his pace to keep up with my longer strides. Over my shoulder I called for the other kids to stay away. The boys near me screamed, too: "Don't go!" I didn't wait to find out if my warning helped—I pulled John away from the filthy truck, into the shadows of the brick, stone, and wood structures.

At first, I just ran, blind. My feet took me down unfamiliar streets, darting between houses, pushing past startled people as I rounded corners, trying to put that truck as far away from me and John as I could. Once the spike of fear faded, John and I caught our breath and navigated through the streets until we found our way toward home. We went straight to our family, and never returned to fetch water from that well.

When kids were abducted, the rebels would turn them into child soldiers. It *is* a terrible thing that they do: kidnaping young boys and giving them drugs to make them dependent and to manipulate them. Then they give them a gun. They make the kids start killing. When—if—the kids ever come back again, they are different. I say, "*is* a terrible thing" because this sort of thing still happens to this day. God protected John and I that day—if we weren't paying attention, we easily could have been abducted and forced to join the rebel groups. Some of the kids who were there that day were never heard from again. We were no different or any more special than any one of those kids. All I can say is that God protected us.

Mom was caring for eight children on her own. We only heard from Dad every few months. Whenever he would call, we would all pack tight around Mom, trying to hear, bouncing up and down waiting for our turn. It was reassuring to hear his voice, but I could hear the distance weighing on him.

I would hear Mom quietly assuring Dad that God was taking care of us. Dad was frustrated. In his mind, the process should have been much faster—a few weeks not months that turned into years. He would tell her that he was tired of staying away without any sign that he was on the right path. Dad would talk about just giving up and coming home; at least we could be together then. Mom was strong, her voice calm. She would tell Dad to be patient and that God was going to come through for us.

I knew Dad was doing everything he could to get us back—he even explained to me that he was trying to get our family added to his documentation and that the refugee agency was just so slow—but it was still hard. When your stomach is groaning, it's hard to think about much else. We were going a day or two without a meal almost every week. People were struggling, starving, all across Bukavu—I saw them begging for food in the streets, their clothes hanging loose on their wiry bodies. But something about Mom's posture helped me not to be destroyed by worry. It was not easy, but I started to feel the confidence inside me that she showed—confidence rooted in trust in God, even when it didn't make sense.

Sometimes Mom would wake me up in the night, shaking me just enough to pry my eyes open a crack so that I would see the outline of her face above me. She would whisper, careful not to wake my brothers. She would ask me to pray with her. Even though sleep weighed me down, like chains on my bed, I would shake it off and swing my legs off the bed. Together, we would glide over to the main room. We'd kneel next to each other on the cold, hard floor. Mom and I would pray, unleashing all of our fears and worry and pain and doubt into the pool of black. In the dark, just me and her, hand-in-hand, I felt God's arms wrapping us in a warm blanket. I knew He was with us. On some nights we would light a candle, and I would peek through my scrunched eyes and watch the faint orange ripples tracing the curves of Mom's face, her round cheeks glowing in the delicate light. She never wore makeup. Her dark curls were cropped tight above her head. Mom never fussed over her appearance, but she was—and remains—lovely. Never more lovely than when she was talking to God. Mom gripped my hand tight in hers as we prayed—I knew she needed someone there with her.

Our money was drying up faster than the roads after rainy season. As much as I tried to provide, my little peanut business was not making enough to support the entire family—a few meals but not every day. It was hard resisting my screaming stomach while I carried armloads of protein around all day.

When we were living day-by-day, hoping to hear from Dad and staring into an empty kitchen as if our eyes could fill it, Heaven sent a knock on our door. Outside, an older woman from church, hair wrapped up in the traditional fashion, stood at our door. Her slim arms were buckling under the weight of a large brown sack—it was filled with rice. Outside, she had beans, corn flour, and cooking oil as well, enough to feed all of us for at least a month. Mom hugged her, fighting tears. The woman looked at each of us kids with small, kind eyes. She smiled more than she talked. As she left, she grabbed me and one of the other boys by the hand and had the rest of the family join us to pray.

God used the woman to help feed us for eight months.

All this time, things in the Congo were deteriorating. The uncertainty haunted us—would rebels show up and force themselves into our home? Would my brothers be abducted? After two years displaced inside our own borders, separated from Dad, we received a visit from another Good Samaritan.

The thickset woman carried herself with rigid posture and dressed very sharp—a bright, traditional dress worn with a crisp poise. She was clearly a businesswoman. Right away she told us that Dad had sent her to bring us to him. I almost fell over. Excitement slammed my chest, making it difficult to say anything understandable at first. With a warm smile, the kind that closes deals, the woman explained that she knew the route to where Dad was in Kenya quite well—she traveled for work often—and that she had agreed to help our family journey there.

We didn't even bother staying another night in the unfriendly apartment. Mom had family near the Rwandan border, so we packed up our few belongings and spent the night with them. All of us were too excited to sleep. We prayed. And we spent time celebrating with loved ones. Aunts, uncles, and cousins chatted with us through the night, laughing as they told stories of when we were smaller, and when they were younger. The men would rest a hand on my shoulder and offer advice on how to be safe on the road, what kind of people to watch out for. The women passed the young girls around, using their free hands to touch me and my brother's faces as they marveled at how much we had grown.

There was a heaviness to the air as well. I did not know if I would ever see any of these people, my people, again. My extended family wore their doubt visibly. Their guarded posture, the way their eyes wouldn't meet ours for long, reminded me they weren't coming with us. They asked us if we were sure we knew what we were doing. They viewed the cage of fear Bukavu built around them as a safety net, comfortable. The ever-present threats from the war were not enough, in their minds, to brave the unknown dangers beyond the Congo's borders. Still, it was a happy sendoff—I was surrounded by smiles, faces that I knew and loved. The violent cracks in the distance shattered any disappointment I may have had at leaving all of them behind.

Bukavu hid under shadows, a golden halo above my motherland as we left the next morning. My feet were quick, purposeful with each step as I crossed the international bridge to Rwanda. Beneath me, Kivu stirred. The waves licked the air as they rippled back to the Congo. Like flames. I kept going, not sure when I would be back but certain I wanted to leave. I felt like I was coming out of Hell.

Chapter Seven

"We Did Not Come Here to Die"
2002-2003

The bus gleamed white on the outside; inside it was plush and smelled new. I couldn't see out the window very well, because my family was crammed in the middle, but red roofs and green patches of trees flashed by, padding the distance between us and the war. The tires spit a cloud of dust over the world we had left behind—the world of terror and bloodshed, of rape, of fear, of heartache. Of evil.

Sometimes I think back, remembering my motherland disappearing behind me, and I am left breathless. It's hard knowing that I made it while others did not. But I am thankful, in a very sober way, that I escaped.

We only had enough money for three seats. The Good Samaritan sat with Asi in her lap, Mom held Adili and Naomi, and I shared a seat with Baraka. John and Christian sat on the floor. A kind stranger offered to take Priscilla and held her the entire ride. The bus was full, but the people smiled and shared stories with us during the trip.

While playing under the seats, Christian and John discovered a box of bananas that had been stored down there. My brothers tore into that stash, leaving the crumpled peels to brown on the floor. They were a sight—two skinny little refugee boys scrunched under the seat, mouths stuffed with yellow fruit. When the woman who owned the bananas discovered them, my brothers' eyes almost popped out of their heads. She just laughed, too taken by their thin, hungry faces to be upset.

I could feel the pull right, then left, as the bus took sharp curves and alternated between steady upward and downward climbs for most of the thirteen-hour journey. It was night when we reached Kigali, Uganda. We spent the night in a hotel near the bus station. I slept easier knowing we were about four hundred seventy miles away from home and knowing no guns would cry out overhead that night.

The next day zipped by; I hardly noticed the steady vibrations from the tires rolling over the smooth pavement. It was another full day of riding, about four hundred miles, crossing up through Uganda, bending around Lake Victoria and into Kenya. Then it was on south, to Nairobi, Kenya's capital city.

It was evening when we arrived in Nairobi. I couldn't see the city over the tan, square buildings that boxed the bus station. It was loud, music blaring from shops all around and people walking by one another in every direction. I felt overwhelmed. I didn't pay much attention to what was going on around me because I was so tired; my eyes were heavy, and my legs were going numb.

When the bus pulled up, the Good Samaritan told us to look out the window. Standing there, arms waving, was Dad. The girls started screaming with excitement and us kids all rushed for the door, pushing against the crowd of bodies. Someone above me yelled to the people in front, "Let the kids come through." We exploded through the door—which felt smaller than when we had stepped on the bus—and pounced on Dad. His arms seemed endless, enough room to hug each of us at the same time. Tears streamed down his face. I didn't try to stop my own; crying, in that moment, washed away all of the fear and uncertainty of the past two years. I felt safe. Our family was united, once again. It was one of the best moments of my life.

More than eight hundred and seventy miles separated me from the Congo. As we crammed into a taxi, riding through Nairobi to our new home, the contrast between where I was and where I had come from struck me. Bukavu at night was overwhelmed by black, drowning any speckles of light, a city of darkness. In Nairobi, we stepped out of the darkness into a pool of light. Cars zoomed by. Electric beams flashed all around, reflecting off windows, climbing high up into the night, illuminating the massive skyscrapers. The skyline felt like a wall of protection.

I felt like all of my problems and struggles had disappeared, buried far beyond the glowing city. My eyelids sagged. Nighttime was bright, but in my mind so was the new life ahead of me.

I did not yet understand the hardships of refugee life.

At first, I was grateful just to be in a safe environment. We settled in the outskirts of Nairobi. Our apartment complex was a series of eggshell stone slabs, arranged in an irregular pattern so that going through them was like winding through a maze. The complex housed refugees from several countries, including Ethiopia, Somalia, and my motherland. Tall, tan buildings looked down on us, depressed windows like eyes stared from every direction.

Our family crammed into a ten-by-ten room—I've stayed in motel rooms bigger than it—which was all we could afford. It was the smallest room in the building. There was a single window that allowed in enough sunlight to drive the shadows into puddles in the corners. At night, we had to use candles. We shared a bathroom with six other families, and to get to it we had to go outside and follow the zig-zagging wall.

I felt like a sardine in a can. We all slept on the floor. Mom and Dad divided the room in two using a curtain. My parents had one side and us kids laid on the other side, four boys sleeping in one direction, the four girls sleeping in the other direction. We used rags as sleeping mats. In the morning, we rolled up our limp, ragged beds so that we had some floor space.

It didn't take long for my hope to get snuffed out by the walls pressing in on all four sides. I would long to feel my legs sprinting across the open field again, our house blocking everything else in sight as you drew closer. I could smell stew simmering over the coals right in the yard as my mind wandered inside. But even as I missed our life in the Congo, I was still haunted by the fear that drove us out.

I remember lounging around inside with my siblings, around eight o'clock one night. We had been living in Kenya for about six months. A thundering ripple of explosions burst out over the city. I was breathless, terrified. I hugged myself into a ball and prayed. Images flooded my mind—blood-soaked bodies, green uniforms, arms casually cradling instruments of death—as shadows flickered behind the candlelight. My brothers pressed in next to me, and we just watched the door, wide-eyed. I was afraid the war had chased us to Kenya.

After about half an hour, Dad went outside to find out what was going on. He came back inside and told us it was just fireworks. People were celebrating the New Year. I was so overwhelmed, my body burning with adrenaline, that I melted onto the hard floor. When I regained my strength, I went outside and watched the lights pop in the sky. Bright colors sprayed a gold-black canvas and then evaporated. It was too much—all I heard were the sounds. I went back inside and covered my ears.

There were nights when I woke up in a cold sweat, heart pounding, shaking off the nightmares. Combat boots would crash the ground outside the doorway, guns would spray bullets and blood across the dirt roads, children would scream for long-gone parents. Then I'd be alone, in the dark, catching my breath. Only, I would realize, I wasn't alone. Feeling John's foot tangled in my legs or Christian's arm across my chest would remind me where I was.

It was hard to keep up when the Kenyan children spoke. My own Swahili was muddied with French—that's how we spoke it in Bukavu, mixed up. Kenya's was pure Swahili. I felt like an outsider every time I opened my mouth. My accent gave me away. I couldn't get my tongue to bend just right to pronounce the words the way the native kids did. So, I was quiet, at first.

Me and my siblings went to a school that was very welcoming to refugees, which helped me to make friends, both with natives and outsiders, like me. Over time, my mouth began to move in smooth rhythm with the Kenyan way of speaking and it helped me to feel more at home. I also learned English.

We were granted refugee status through the United Nations High Commissioner for Refugees (UNHCR). This gave us legal protection. However, Dad was not allowed to work. With ten mouths to feed and no income, the savings my parents had from selling everything in Bukavu drained in less than a year.

Throughout our years in Kenya, God showed up in a big way—He provided for us day after day, sometimes in ways that I cannot even explain.

Mom would wash clothes to help provide money for our family. She scrubbed her hands raw in a wooden bucket, suds spilling out over her feet, for a full day, only to earn one hundred Kenyan shilling—the equivalent of about one U.S. dollar.

There was this Kenyan woman that Mom worked for who seemed very nice at the start. But the woman soon started to act strange, making excuses to not pay for Mom's work or demanding more work for less money. She talked down to Mom and made it seem like she would cause problems for us legally if Mom tried to argue.

I could see that Mom was unhappy, the way she kept her eyes down when she handed the fresh, folded clothes over without receiving the handful of coins she was promised in return. But Mom kept her mouth closed. She held her frustration inside until later, when she would drop to her knees, head bowed against her fists, and pour it all out to God. I never heard her complain once. And Mom never let her face give away what she had just unleashed to Heaven. But God hears the prayers of a righteous follower.

One weekend, I remember the woman came around looking for Mom as I was still laying on the floor, wedged between two siblings. My mom carefully stepped over us, trying not to wake anyone up as she answered the door. I didn't have to look up to know what was going on—I heard that the woman was sobbing uncontrollably. I peeked up anyway and saw Mom patting the woman's arm, trying to comfort her, asking what was going on. When the woman managed to control her breathing enough for words to spill out, she said, "I had a dream about you. God showed me your life and how I have been treating you unfairly just because you are a refugee. God warned me never to do that again, telling me, 'This is my servant; have some respect.'"

From where I lay, I could see that she was shaking as she spoke. I saw dread in her eyes. She promised to never act that way again. Mom just hugged her and then looked her in the eye and offered forgiveness.

After that day, the woman would bring her bundle of clothes with a smile. She even brought us some food from time-to-time. I could see on her face that God worked in that woman's heart, and she displayed it with her generosity, paying my mom better from then on.

Money was so tight for us for about a year that my parents could only afford cornmeal and kale. So, every single day that's what we ate—bitter kale leaves and bland, gritty cornmeal. My siblings and I complained, like the Israelites in the desert receiving their daily manna. My face crumpled in disgust when I shoveled down the plain food. I always emptied my plate; I needed whatever fuel my body could get. But I craved meat, like an outcast lion wandering the wilderness. On my way home from school, or out playing in the paved streets, I'd catch the scent of fresh meat, distracting me from whatever I was doing. I would stalk the butcher shops, staring at the juicy, pink slabs through the window.

Me and my siblings constantly battled the symptoms of *Kwashiorkor*, a form of malnutrition[10] stemming from severe protein deficiency. We weren't getting the protein and fats in our diet needed to feel strong and gain weight. Priscilla, Adili, Asi, Naomi and Esther especially suffered from stunted growth in Kenya.

While I started growing taller, I could also feel my ribs pressing out of my sides. My brothers were bone-thin as well. Most of the time I felt weak—when I got home from school I would lean against a hard, cool wall in the shadows watching the other kids run up and down the street. Longing to join, but lacking the strength, I would close my eyes and drift into a place between being awake and asleep. My groaning stomach would remind me it was empty.

Even as we faced this sickness, day in and day out, God provided for us, often in surprising ways. Just like when the Lord sent ravens with food to Elijah in exile.

One day, Dad was sitting outside, his belly growling loud as he tried talking to God. A hearty meal, bundled in burnt orange feathers, strutted by. The rooster's crest flapped carelessly as it walked right on by my dad. As he watched it peck at the ground, Dad said to himself,

This chicken looks good. But it wasn't like Dad could just take someone else's chicken. It was just a passing thought, while he was praying like he always did. But God heard Dad anyway.

Nothing is too big, or even too small—something as unremarkably common in America as a chicken dinner—for our Lord. He provides. God blesses us by giving us just enough to get by, and, at other times, by giving us beyond what we could imagine.

When Dad got home, he found Mom in the middle of our small room, firing up our kerosene cooker. She hummed to herself as she collected the few ingredients we had for dinner. Again, it was cornmeal and kale.

The table we had in our apartment was just big enough for Mom's cooker and a couple pots and pans. Just like every other evening, we all grabbed our plates and found a spot on the floor. I may not have been thrilled for what I would taste, but I was ready to eat. Once we were all assembled and Dad was about to pray for our meal, there was a knock at the door. I watched as Dad opened the door, revealing a tall, muscular Kenyan man. I recognized his wide, gleaming smile—the Kenyan man would always say hello if I passed him going to work. The clean-cut man kept his face baby smooth, hair cropped tight, and wore modern clothes; a pressed button shirt hung loose over his chiseled frame, tucked into slacks.

When he stepped through the doorway, I saw that the man was carrying a large bowl. "I slaughtered my chicken, but I could not finish it all," he announced. His delivery was direct, to the point. "I only ate one piece; I felt in my heart that I should bring the rest for you guys." He did not look like the type of man who only ate one piece of chicken, no matter how fat and juicy that chicken was. And this was one of the fattest and juiciest I've ever had.

Me and the other kids cheered, jumping up off the bare floor. We started hugging his legs. After he left, I was ravenous and didn't even think before reaching for the bowl. But Dad stopped us. "Wait a minute, wait a minute, children," he scolded. "Before we even eat this chicken, let me tell you the story about it." He went on to tell us, in more words than my stomach cared for, about his silent prayer earlier that day. For a moment, the pains inside stilled; I was blown away. I knew that day that God saw us. To me, that little bit of chicken was a miracle.

Days like that helped my faith grow stronger. As my family's hardships continued, I began telling God how I felt instead of just emptying my mind in hopes the struggle would pass. I would tell God that I wanted to eat meat. And He started providing.

There was this thin woman with lighter brown skin who owned a butcher shop. She stayed at home with her kids and had employees who ran the store. I remember it had only been open for a few weeks, maybe months. I noticed it when the scent hit me unexpectedly, driving my mouth to water.

One day the woman just appeared outside our house with several pounds of beef. I never saw her with meat, but there she was in a white, blood-stained apron over her dress, carrying more meat than she had on her own body. I was surprised at how easily she managed the load.

She called out to my Mom, saying, "I couldn't sell this; nobody was buying. So, I thought about you guys."

Over the next few weeks, we ate meat like never before. Mom prepared a rich stew one night and grilled up some savory strips for us another. She also dried out some of the beef, so that it lasted longer.

After that, I stopped complaining and I even got to a point where I *wanted* to eat kale again. God's power was displayed to me and my family through His provision. His blessings overflowed.

During the hardest times, when we had nothing, I remember Dad used to repeat one phrase. Sometimes he would say it to all of us, when we were holding hands in our tiny room, praying for a meal we didn't have. We always had prayers, whether we had dinner or not. Or he'd say it when I was getting discouraged, feeling like we were trapped with nowhere to go and nothing to do but just die. His preacher face would come on—his eyes would harden, his face would draw in, but his mouth moved like silk. There was a tenderness in the deep rolling of Dad's voice; he cared about how you felt, and he also believed with firm conviction in what he was saying. He would insist, "We did not come here to die." If it was just us talking, Dad would grip my shoulder and tell me to be encouraged. "God brought you here. You are not going to die." To the whole family he would say, "We didn't come from afar, God didn't protect us on that journey for us to die here."

"We did not come here to die," he would repeat.

I didn't see a way out, but Dad's words helped me to hold on in faith. Mom started using the phrase, too. She believed that if we trusted Him, God had a purpose for us.

The other refugees who lived in our building or nearby started giving up. Many families left, heading back to the Congo or other countries even though they had been driven out by war. Sometimes, I would hear them talking to my dad. They would ask him why we wouldn't take our family back, perhaps to feel better because they felt hopeless. Dad would respond with a frozen expression, words like ice in the heat of day, "If my God tells me to go back, then I will go. But he has not told me to."

Rooms would empty, one after the other, only to be filled by new families. So many gave up. The ones who stayed did so with a cloud of hopelessness over them.

My family had nobody else but God.

After surviving on small meals for quite some time, maybe a few weeks, I remember running out of food completely. The church where we relied on for dry goods stopped distributing food to refugees. All of my family's resources dried up. We didn't eat a bite for two days. I couldn't play anymore; I would just wander over to a field and lie down on my back, sinking into the grass, watching the sky devour clouds. I had no strength left.

With ten of us and not a bite between us, I remember getting home to hear Mom say, "I have nothing to feed you all, but I know God is able to provide."

She had all of us cross our legs and circle around the room like we always did before dinner. Mom handed each of us our plate. Then, she set down her cooking pans, which rang hollow against the table. From where I was sitting, it looked like pure insanity. Like the hunger had driven her mad.

Mom started praying. I felt the cool, dead weight of my plate in my hand. Its surface was smooth against my palm, bare. But Mom's words bounced off every empty dish with power. In my childish faith, I started to believe that food might fall from the sky at any moment. Mom's faith was grounded, her face lifted up toward Heaven. She kept telling God that she knew that He saw us, that he had the strength to provide. I started praying, too. The words gushed out like a raging river. I heard my siblings crying out, too. We laid our hands on our empty plates and prayed over them. Our voices filled the emptiness, fully trusting in God's power.

We started singing praises. Dripping with passion, the notes echoed across the hollow pots. We carried on for nearly an hour. It was crazy faith. I started to think maybe we had all lost our minds.

It was an emotional experience, but it was not pleasant. The plates stayed empty. As I laid my heart on the floor, letting all of myself go, nothing came inside to fill me back up—at least not my stomach.

I remember Mom reciting the same phrase Dad used, "God did not bring us here to die." It stung my ears.

Despite Dad's faith, despite Mom's faith, despite all of our faith, no manna came to our plates from Heaven.

When we were all exhausted, our songs faded to heavy gasps for breath, and my parents excused us. As I darkened the doorframe to leave, my siblings right behind me, Mom told us she did not want any of us kids going out knocking on people's doors begging for food. I left the house no fuller than when I had come in.

I forced my weary body around a corner and collapsed against the wall. Other kids were playing in the street, but I did not want to do anything. I was wasting time. I didn't think about anything, I just sulked, staring out into the distance. The sun grew heavier, the gray stone behind me colder, and I started to believe that I could smell a meal, winding through the air, inviting me to get up.

When I finally picked myself up and dragged my feet toward our room, the smell grew stronger. Outside my door, it was attacking my nostrils. When I walked inside, I found Mom cooking. Everyone else was already back inside, beaming smiles at me. I couldn't believe my eyes.

As her hands danced around the table, Mom explained that while I was gone there was a knock at the door. God sent a woman to our house with cooking oil, beans, and rice—enough to feed us all for four days.

Faith had moved a mountain.

"See, I told you that God would provide." Mom dropped the words on top of the spoonful she heaped on my plate.

Before we could touch the food, however, Mom reminded us of Jesus' words in Matthew 6, where Christ pointed to the birds of the air, always cared for by our Father in Heaven. "Are you not of more value than they?" Jesus asked. "Which of you by worrying can add one cubit to his stature?" (NKJV).

I realized—as I swallowed down mouthfuls without bothering to chew—that there's nothing God can't do and with Him all is possible.

That night, my family and I had a feast—in our minds at least. The food wasn't extravagant or rich, but it was life giving. We praised God with each bite. I could feel His power filling me up, the strength sinking deeper than my stomach, my muscles, my bones. I felt it in my soul.

I am living proof that God still performs miracles in the world.

Chapter Eight
Waiting Up for Mom
2003

Silver darts of moonlight stabbed my eyes. It was around midnight. I looked up in time to see Mom disappear through the door, into the darkness. Even with swollen ankles carrying her ripe belly, she stepped delicately. I hadn't even felt her brush over me when she tiptoed through the entangled bodies of me and my siblings, cramped in our tiny half of the room, to check on us before she left. I assumed she was going to the bathroom.

I waited for her to come back, but she never did. Not that night.

Sometime in the night Mom started having labor pains. There was nowhere to go—we lived on the outskirts of town. Even the refugee camps, though the living conditions were worse than where we lived, had better access to medical care. Mom knew that there was no way she would make it to a hospital, so she whispered to Dad, "I'm going to have my baby right here," and left the apartment.

Dad rushed out right behind her. The owner of our compound was a nurse, so Dad leaned Mom against his arm and walked her over to the landlady's door. He pounded his fist on the wood, frantic. He called out through the window. Mom saw faces appear, then vanish. No one came out to help.

My mom is such a strong woman. Gritting through the pain, she told Dad that she did not want to disturb her other children. So, she walked away from the compound, settling by a fence that surrounded another property, leaving the eight of us sprawled out on the floor.

With no idea what was happening, I leaned up on my elbows and watched the door. Dad burst back inside, grabbed a rug and a lamp, and marched back outside. His words rode the air to us as the door whooshed shut: "Stay in prayer. Mom is about to have the baby."

I didn't see or hear anything else for three hours. I couldn't sleep, so I just watched the dark shapes that filled the stillness before me. My eyes kept telling me something had shifted, a flutter of shadow, a sign that someone was coming with good news, or bad news, any news. But it was just the night playing its tricks on me.

Mom took the mat from Dad and laid it on the flat dirt outside. She didn't want to be surrounded by the eyes of our neighbors. But, just beyond the fence where she settled were seven wild dogs. These were not pets at all. The matted, golden-brown mutts had disease-ridden mouths filled with sharp, pointed teeth that snapped at anything that got near the fence. I remember the chorus of barking that erupted when you walked by, followed by low, angry growls. The owners kept those dogs for security. Sometimes, they didn't feed the dogs just to keep them angry. There were times when the owners were away that the dogs would get out. I'd hear them sniffing around the streets, claws scratching against the pavement, snarling at anyone who tried to walk out onto the street.

Dad was in charge of watching out for the dogs while Mom struggled through her contractions. On the ground, with just a beat-up rug for support and an old sheet spread at her feet, Mom pushed. She only had faint, yellow torchlight and the moon overhead to see by.

Two Kenyan neighbors heard the commotion outside and, when they realized what was happening, came running across the street to help my mom. They were young women—their faces were smooth and bright: one a deep ebony the other a creamy coffee. Each had two children of their own, though they hardly looked old enough. The women helped Mom through the birth.

I heard footsteps, real ones this time, and one of the women appeared through our door. She carried a sheet, bundled up and cradled in her arms. As my eyes adjusted to the change in light—now dull purple with rusty ripples staining the black—I saw that there was a baby wrapped in the cloth. The woman carefully unwrapped the newborn and swaddled her in a fresh blanket.

Dad came in without a word a few minutes later. He dug through some papers, stuffing Mom's refugee documentation into his pocket. By then, morning's gold waves were floating in. When Dad turned to whisper to the woman, I saw that his shirt, once white, was soaked red. It seemed he was out of the room before I even realized he had come in. The woman and the baby were gone as well.

For me, the whole night and the next day were just flashes: Dad coming and going. These appearances happened over several hours. But the waiting, the long hours, just melted into nothing. Everything in between, when my parents were gone, had been skipped over. And I had no idea what was going on. I'm not sure if I could have handled all of that empty silence if I knew what was happening.

After the birth, things got out of control. Mom kept losing blood. Her placenta was stuck. While the one neighbor brought the baby to our room, the other sprinted to get her friend who drove a taxi. A pool of blood covered the ground around where Mom lay. Dad didn't waste a second, not even to tell me what was going on, when he bolted across the street, charged in and out of the apartment, and ran right back. He lifted Mom's limp body into the waiting taxi. Mom was conscious, but still hemorrhaging. With the baby in his arms, he jumped in the car and accompanied her to the hospital.

It was an hourlong ride to Pumwani Maternity Hospital. Back then, the healthcare system in Kenya was a mess. It was not like what you would expect in the States—everything moved at a snail's pace. People would die while waiting to see a doctor.

When the taxi pulled up to the glass entrance doors, no one came outside. Nurses looked on while Dad sprinted to grab a flat cart for Mom. She was like a sack of meat, bloody and lifeless as Dad struggled to heave her onto the gurney. The nurses just watched. They shook their heads as if they already knew she wouldn't make it.

Dad waved his hands, demanding that they do something, until Mom and the baby were whisked deep into the glowing white gut of the building. Once they were fully absorbed by the brightness, Dad stood solid, like a rock, unable to move. Silently, deep within his soul, he cried out. No sound escaped his lips, just heavy gasps for breath. Dad's body released and began to shake. He cried, dry sobs, begging God, "Don't take my wife, don't take my wife, not yet, not yet!" He prayed, "You are the healer, God—heal my wife and bring her back to us. Have mercy, oh God! We did not come here to die in Kenya!"

Outside, alone, crying in desperation, Dad wondered how he could care for all of us on his own. He had no idea what was happening inside the hospital, but he trusted God.

Dad's white shirt was still covered with blood. People passed by and, when they noticed him, went pale, looking at him horrified, as if he had just killed someone.

An hour passed before a doctor came running out. He told my dad not to panic and that Mom was still hanging on. But she needed blood. Dad almost forgot to wait for the doctor to show him the way after bounding forward with an, "I'm ready," and pushing through the door.

He let the nurses draw as much blood as they needed. Dad would have let them drain him dry if they wanted to. Then, with a soft white bandage squeezing the inside of his arm, Dad waited, still wearing the stains from holding on for Mom's life. Dad could hardly sit. Sleep haunted him, but his mind raced ahead of it. He alternated sitting, with his face buried in his hands, and pacing nervously back and forth. Only his fading strength from giving blood finally forced him to sit.

When the doctor emerged, he wore a relieved expression. But he spoke carefully, as if to emphasize how serious the situation was. The doctor started by confessing that he was ready to pronounce Mom dead when she came through the door.

"She was gone, but," the doctor paused, indicating that he had no medical explanation for what happened, "God brought her back."

The news sent Dad flying to his feet. He jumped for joy, crying, "Thank you Jesus!"

It was mid-afternoon when Dad finally came home to deliver the news. He was disheveled, eyes puffy from sleep deprivation, still wearing that blood-stained shirt. The sour stench of old sweat clung to him. Through the mess, however, Dad was radiating his relief and gratitude. Whatever anxiety I had felt that day disappeared the moment I learned Mom was OK. She meant everything to us. And God had rescued her from the brink of death. Our family saw firsthand that nothing can stop the Almighty God—nothing is over until He says it is over.

It was three days before Mom came home from the hospital with the baby girl—my sister, Esther. I remember holding Esther in my arms. Cradling her was like holding a pillow; she was so tiny, soft, and light. As her oldest brother, I felt a weight of responsibility when I held her. I wished she could have been born in a different place, at a different time. A time like when we were carefree in Bukavu, before the war. I wanted a better life for her, and it made me feel as helpless as she was—there was nothing I could do for her. Well, almost nothing. I gave her my love. We all did. To this day, we consider Esther our miracle baby. She brought great rejoicing to our family in the midst of so much hardship.

Chapter Nine

The Congo Boys
2003-2008

I used to walk for forty-five minutes to one of the city parks in Nairobi. Toddler-sized monkeys—black, with white scarves of fur hanging off their necks and shoulders—swung through the tangled branches above, the thick wall of trees providing plenty of cool shade. They walked right up to people begging for food. The grass grew in patches, beaten bare from frequent visitors. I felt the grains of dirt rubbing into my soles as I played soccer with my friends. My shoes were falling apart around my feet.

When I left my motherland, I was a boy, just entering my teenage years. But I already felt the burden of manhood. I had cared for my family while Dad was seeking out a safe place for all of us. I believed Kenya was going to be the end of the struggle, but my life quickly became a daily fight for survival. Even with Dad around, I carried a weight on my shoulders as I felt the need to help care for my eight siblings. I felt like I had missed much of my childhood.

I often looked back to one Christmas morning in 1999, a couple of years after my family had returned to Bukavu from Kaziba. I was ten. We weren't expecting any presents that year—war had made business tight for my dad. So, when Dad told me to reach under my chair, and I felt plastic crinkling against my fingers, I was too cautious to be excited. I pulled the shopping bag into my lap and put my hand inside, pulling out a fresh pair of sneakers. I traced the untainted white stripes along the smooth, black surface. My first pair of shoes.

I didn't mind going barefoot when I was younger, but the burning pain I felt from contracting jiggers in the village was seared in my memory. Pulling the soft fabric over my dirt-crusted feet melted that anxiety away. I felt the soft cushion hugging my arches, cradling my soles. They were a little too big—my legs looked like they were being swallowed up—but, to me, the shoes felt secure. I was able to just enjoy Christmas without worrying about the war that was clashing all around me, tearing my city apart. I felt safe. I had been given something new, something that was mine. I had hope.

I grew into my shoes quickly, but it wasn't long before they were shrinking around my feet. Still, as I rode the bus through Rwanda and Uganda to Nairobi. I clung to that hope tightly on the journey. Facing new struggles in a foreign land, I wore those shoes ragged, until my toes stuck out of the frayed material. My hope transferred to another pair, bought before my parents were worried about our savings disappearing.

I didn't always feel the hope, but I carried it with me—on my feet. Sometimes just slipping on the worn fabric—pulling the laces tight against me, feeling the synthetic rubber align beneath my weight—

reminded me that I was protected. I remembered Jesus' words in Matthew, that the Lord saw to it that even the flowers of the field had clothes. And I felt God looking out for me.

Running out in the open air of the park, with Nairobi's cityscape poking the sky in the background, was my escape. I wasn't just a refugee there; I was a teammate. There was nothing to fight for except possession of the soccer ball. But as I missed a pass, the ball spinning into the open grass ahead as I tripped forward, half my foot sticking through the bottom of my shoe, I felt like I was done. I kicked the mesh corpses off and chased after the other kids. Hope had a way of wearing out. God, however, always had more to give.

I started walking around barefoot. The bottoms of my feet were beaten raw by the hard asphalt roads, but my skin calloused in defense.

Instead of allowing my soul to harden, too, I decided to surrender my problems to the Lord. At a church prayer meeting where I joined my parents with the other grown-ups, I remember dropping to my knees and asking for God's provision out loud. The others crowded around me; I felt their hands on my back and shoulders and knew more were extended out toward me. It was reassuring—more comforting than the feeling of lacing up a pair of shoes.

I didn't realize then that it was that moment—kneeling down and praying for God to provide me with a pair of shoes—that would define my future. One day, I was going to be the answer to that same prayer. I would be providing shoes for children in the Congo and across Africa. Me, a barefoot refugee. God works in mysterious ways and, truly, our destiny is in His hands.

Weeks went by and my feet remained naked. While the bumps and cracks in the ground tried to wear at my faith, they only served to reinforce the strength of my soles.

I wasn't forced to draw closer to God as we faced hardship; it was a choice. By watching my parents, I learned to trust God, even when things felt hopeless. I never once heard them curse God or doubt His ability to help us. This shaped my personal growth, making me who I am today. I became a man in Kenya.

About a year after Esther was born, we had moved into a new place, a small house with a separate bedroom for my parents. One evening, I remember finding Dad paralyzed in the living room. He was frozen in his chair. His eyes were wide, but he did not move his arms or legs. Even when I touched him, Dad didn't respond. I felt my own nerves seizing up because I was so frightened. Tears flooded my face, my chest heaving—I literally cried to God because I didn't know what else to do.

I yelled out the window until my neighbors came and called for help. As soon as my mom left to take Dad to the hospital, I pulled myself together. I had to be strong for the little ones. I pooled all my siblings in the main room, hands clasped tightly together, just like Mom and Dad always did with us. I led the family in prayer, asking God for his hand of healing to touch my dad. Even after the younger kids fell asleep, one by one, I kept praying. Priscilla and Adili collapsed as the night wore on. Christian almost managed to make it through the night. John and Baraka were by my side casting words up to Heaven, as sunlight crept through the window.

Mom told me the next day that a man approached her in the hospital, late into the night, while I had been praying. The man spoke her tribal language. He announced that God sent him to her. He assured her, before he just got up and walked out of the hospital, that "God said your husband would not die. That man still has work to do for the Lord."

At the hospital, Dad miraculously regained his strength. The feeling flooded back into his body, flowing to his fingers and toes, which he wiggled on command as the doctors examined him. They could not find anything wrong with him. The doctors kept him until the morning before they released him—no diagnosis, no recommended treatment. He was completely healed.

Whenever I covered the distance between school or the park on foot, my steps often painted an irregular pattern. Two or three normal steps, then five or six short, quick thumps, followed by a leap, a sidestep, and another stride. My feet were following the beat in my head. If John, Baraka, and Christian were with me, they'd dance along, and we would sing our favorite songs from church, putting a Congolese *seben* spin on the Kenyan tunes. Unlike our time in Bukavu, when we only tolerated church music and idolized the stars of music videos, we were inspired by Christian music. We started to choreograph routines to the songs.

One day, while my sore, bare feet were resting, my legs stretched out in front of me on the floor, an answer to prayer appeared at our door. A month on the streets had left its marks on my heels. Outside, a woman, a Congolese refugee like me, waited to give me a gift. In her hands was a pair of shoes. She had seen me wandering around barefoot and felt sympathy for me—so she went and bought me some shoes. I was so overwhelmed with emotion. The sores on my toes left my mind as my fingers stroked the smooth, black leather. I didn't know what to say. "Thank you" was all I could seem to squeeze out, but it didn't feel like enough. God had used her to do a miracle for me.

The next time I was dancing through the streets, I was supported by a thick, sturdy heel. I probably did not turn any heads—maybe wrinkled some eyebrows—since the shoes were not exactly fashionable, but my covered feet made me feel like the whole world saw me. God's blessings were on display, a tough hide of protection to show I was His.

Five years in Kenya helped ease my fear that the war in the Congo would catch up with me. That feeling shattered in 2007.

I remember walking home after an election. The results had been highly disputed, and the entire atmosphere of the city changed. Tension clouded the streets. As people walked by, their eyes wandered nervously.

No one lingered in the streets; they walked rigid lines to where they needed to go and back. Doors closed faster and louder when people disappeared into their homes.

I saw a kid I had played with—a teenager no older than me—sharpening a machete. There was anger burning in his eyes. That boy hardly had any hairs sprouting from his chin; he probably didn't have a razor to shave with. Yet there he was, running his fingers across a blade the length of his arm.

The Kikuyu tribe was in the majority in Kenya. Members of the Jaluo and Luhya tribes—both large but not as big as the Kikuyu—claimed that the majority tribe had rigged the election in their favor. Fights broke out in our neighborhood. People turned on one another, slashing their neighbors, even former friends, to a bloody mess because of their race. Jaluos and Luhyas attacked Kikuyus, claiming they had stolen power. Kikuyus attacked the other tribes for stirring up trouble. It just felt like everyone was attacking one another.

One time, John and I were walking in the street, not bothering anybody, and someone screamed at us, calling us Jaluo. They must have been Kikuyu. They said we looked like *them*. We sprinted home without looking back and did not come out for the rest of the day.

Another time, Dad was taking Christian to buy kerosene and a fight broke out in the streets. Two rival tribes, one on each side of the road, clashed swinging fists and clubs at each other, the force whipping wind around the heads of my dad and brother. Rocks started flying, whizzing through the air, thumping into bodies, striking walls, then rattling on the ground. Dad and Christian had to duck and shove their way out of the riot.

The ethnic violence in Kenya left as many as fifteen hundred people dead[11]. I've always found it heartbreaking how politics can divide people, pitting brother against brother and causing them to turn on one another.

Not everything about my life in Kenya was bad.

At church, with a massive wooden cross overhead, me and my brothers flowed with the beat like fish in water. Natural light poured over the two hundred or so church members as we all sang at the top of our lungs. Not a single body was still; everyone was on their feet, arms raised, hands clapping, hips swaying. That's how it is in African churches; the music isn't the kind you sit for. Even if you wanted to sit, the worship leaders roused the sea of people, stirring the energy as they called out for responses across the room. The time of praise went on for hours.

My favorite Sundays were the ones when Dad preached. He had such a strength in his voice, which boomed across the rectangular room, pulsing through the speakers. *Hallelujahs* and *amens* echoed back in response. Dad's tone shifted easily to allow the still small silence to penetrate hearts with the truth, his words sailing delicately around the pauses. As he delivered God's Word with authority, I felt like even the birds outside stopped cawing. I've always looked up to my dad. I'm the man I am today because of him.

I served on the church's praise team with my brothers. As we rediscovered our passion for music and flair for showmanship, we began to give special performances, just the four of us—me, John, Baraka, and Christian. We choreographed dances to Kenyan praise songs. After a while, we began to sing as well, adding our seben twists to the music. The Congolese sound was a hit—there were several DRC refugees in our church, but even the Kenyans enjoyed our music. Kenyan music has many aggressive rhythms, too, but seben has a unique flavor, deep and smooth.

We started a youth choir at our church. My brothers and I would practice all the time. We were at church almost every day, filling the empty room with joyful thunder. Sometimes kids from church and the surrounding neighborhood would come just to watch us rehearse. We put on a show for them. Unlike when I was in Bukavu, however, the music was not about me. In my maturing faith, I decided that I was going to serve God with my life. Including my music. When my feet caught the fever, and my hands shattered the air, it was a joyful noise to the Lord. And the words were all lifting praises to God.

We called ourselves The Congo Boys. Other churches started inviting us to perform. Our seben spin, sung to familiar, Swahili songs, was a hit. We traveled across the city, leading worship at church services, spiritual revivals, crusades, and youth rallies.

One time, we got a gig at a church conference in another town, Machakos, which was between three or four hours east of where we were living. It was a long way for us to travel without our parents. We were being offered money to perform, which was a blessing during a time when our family was struggling, so Mom and Dad let us go.

There were more than five hundred people at the conference. I could feel the Holy Spirit move through the sea of people as we sang and guide my feet as they darted back and forth across the stage, pounding in time with my brothers.' It was an incredible feeling. The sound of all those voices coming together, rising to Heaven, was beautiful. I didn't even feel the strain of exhaustion until the event was over.

My throat blistered as I packed in tightly beside my brothers on the bus ride home. My eyes were ready to roll back and drag me under.

I remember that the driver was barreling down the highway at an aggressive speed. It was suffocating inside—the bus was full and, as it raced, felt like it was shrinking. Trees zipped by like a moving painting.

Then there was a sudden drop, jolting my body like I had been struck by lightning.

One of the front wheels flew off. My eyes opened wide. It was like the world paused around me; I remember watching the tire rolling across the freeway, sweeping my field of vision. The vehicle lurched forward and slammed on the pavement, skidding off the road. It all happened so fast. My heart was crashing against my ribcage as if it could break free.

In that moment, the driver started screaming at the passengers, "Call on your God!" I remember how me and my brothers cried out, repenting of our sins. Some people were yelling out prayers to Allah. Behind me, others were calling upon the name of Jesus Christ along with me and my brothers. The bus slid off the highway and into the trees as I pleaded for mercy, for protection.

I felt my heart in my throat. I froze. It is a strange feeling when fear kicks in, expelling all other impulses. Adrenaline spikes through your body and your brain zeroes in on the moment. It is hard to describe, but my mind went blank of everything except trusting God. There were really no sensible words forming in my throat except, "Lord save us."

We hit the trees at top speed, tearing through the first trunks we encountered, and eventually collided with a large log that halted us to a full stop, forcibly rattling all the passengers. But everyone in the bus was alive, safe and sound. It was a miracle. My brothers and I praised Jesus for His protection. There were only minor injuries; John had a trickle of blood running from his head down the side of his face, and Baraka's neck was almost too stiff to move.

Speeding toward disaster, watching life pass by frame by frame, as if in slow motion, reminded me that I serve a living God. He will not take you home until you have completed His work, the plan He has orchestrated for you to fulfill. I was thankful that day to be fully covered by the blood of Jesus, the Lamb who takes away the sin of the world.

I was rattled. I was shaken. But I was mostly unharmed. More than anything, I was amazed—I had witnessed God step into my life with yet another miracle.

Chapter Ten

Waiting for Our Angel
2008-2009

W e were stuck. Life in Nairobi wasn't getting any better. One day
my family would have a meal, the next we would not. There
was nothing to go back to in the Congo. My family felt like the
Israelites facing the Red Sea—there was no turning back to Egypt, yet
the raging waters ahead blocked any forward motion. All we could do
was wait upon the Lord. But after one year, then two, and then six had
passed, I began to doubt there was anything else for us.

One day in 2008, Dad sat the family down to share a recent dream
he had. In the night, God had told him, "I've heard your cry, and I have
sent an angel to fight for you." I was so excited that I couldn't close

95

my eyes when we started praying. I assumed things would start turning around right away.

Instead, not long after Dad's dream, our case to be relocated by the UN was rejected. Again.

Dad kept going back. For eight years, he followed our file though the maze of halls at the UNHCR. That was one of the benefits of living where we did—it was only a short walk to the headquarters. He was determined to get our family out of Kenya. Dad marched up to the high cement block wall, which was weathered with charcoal age spots, every few weeks to get the UN employees to dig up our file and keep our family's hope stirring. He kept going back, crossing past the guard, under the spiral barbed wire, until he got an interview. Once he did, he would haul our entire family into a stuffy room—a new one each time, but there were never enough chairs for all of us—where he would disappear behind another door and we would wait and watch the light drain from the windows. He'd emerge with a blank face and we would all go home.

This process dragged on. The vines weaving through the rusted chain link fence outside the walls grew thick and green as Dad would wait for an answer, only to be met with months of silence. Then, another interview. And more silence.

When he got a rejection letter, Dad would go back to the UN and refile our case.

The last rejection letter, not long after my dad's dream in 2008, felt like a crushing blow to me. Dad's persistence was not being rewarded. Our neighbors, the refugees who had not yet given up and gone back to their native countries, watched us proceed out of our house, one-by-one, and shook their heads. They told my parents that our family was too big to have any hope of getting a visa. Dad still kept his head high. I felt like the neighbors must be right. Not one refugee family had been accepted, and we were the largest family by far.

Inside, I felt ready to give up. I just wanted to go back to the Congo. It didn't help that my stomach was spinning—cycling from a meal one day and nothing to eat the next.

I tried not to complain. When my emotions did spill out, I let them surge with raw honesty instead of damming up the truth of what I was feeling and hardening my heart against my parents and God. Still, questions would stream out of my aching chest, "If God sent an angel for us, then why are we getting rejected at every turn?"

Mom would stare into my face, her eyes blazing with belief, and, with a firm, soft voice remind me, "He is fighting." Dad would pat my back, adding, "God does not follow human plans."

But the 2008 rejection letter knocked the wind out of Dad. He started to wonder if God was pushing him in another direction. He applied for asylum in Canada through a small agency that placed refugees all around the world.

The road out of Kenya seemed blocked, but a glimmer of hope shone down this new path. Our documents sailed through each stage of the process. Together, Mom and Dad decided that they needed to focus on this track. Dad decided to stop visiting the UN office.

But after five months, he felt a pull as he was walking and found himself outside the impenetrable walls of the UN office. In his heart, God was telling Dad to go inside.

When the receptionist's fingers rattled "Vincent Ntibonera" across the keyboard, her eyes grew wide. Drawing a hand to her chest, the woman asked, "Where have you been? We have been looking for you!" She stood up to shuffle some papers together.

Dad admitted that he had given up after being dismissed at every turn for the past eight years. "What was I supposed to do?" he asked.

The woman nodded with compassion, laid the papers in Dad's hands and said things would be different this time. She sat back down, keys clacking under a blur of hands. She told Dad to come back the next day. We had an interview. We were being considered for a U.S. visa.

Now light was blinding my parents from two directions. They prayed with all nine of us children every night, asking for God to give us clarity. We were seeing a smooth path to Canada, possibly Australia, if the first application with the smaller agency didn't go through. The agency had just scheduled us for an interview. But the door to the U.S. seemed to have been kicked open by God's design.

There were a few weeks when my parents weighed the decision. Every step with both the UN and the other agency landed unhindered. Eventually our family had to choose which way to go. In our prayer circle, I told my parents that it seemed safer to go with the smaller agency. I couldn't take the endless silence. The new path seemed safer.

Dad let my words sink into the creases around his eyes and mouth. He led us through more prayers and then went into his room with Mom. When he came out, Dad sat back down and told us the story of the Israelites following the Lord to the promised land. Always the preacher.

"God was praised after he made a way where there seemed to be no way," Dad's said, drawing his eyes up. "The most difficult path is the one that gives Him the most glory."

That settled it. We had followed God through the wilderness for eight years. Dad wasn't going to let us wander off. I felt like there was a mountain before us, but my parents helped me remember that the Lord can remove any obstacle.

Dad took a leap of faith, calling the small organization to cancel our interview.

To prepare for our meeting at the U.S. Embassy, my family had to rehearse our story, day after day. We had to be consistent in our interview, even with the smallest details—if you were recalling an event and described yourself wearing a white T-shirt, and then was asked about it again and said you were wearing a red shirt, your case could be canceled. It was tough. My mind felt like fufu each day after Dad tested us, throwing questions on top of each other.

We had a two-hour preliminary interview with a European man. He kept pressing me on things that had happened eight, nine, ten years earlier, even as far back as the 1990s, when I was just a kid. At this point I was almost twenty. I kept messing up. Details were fuzzy; it had been so long and so much had happened since. But the man looked at me with understanding. He told me not to be scared—he said that he was here to help my family with our case. He was helping clarify the details in our documents so that our case would be ready for the Embassy.

I felt like I was seeing the angel, fighting for us, right in front of me. I had been coasting on my parents' faith for so long. Now, I believed.

The night before our main interview, our family sang. Our little house filled with deep, heartfelt spirituals, all of our voices blending together as if they were one tongue. Each of us closed our eyes tight and let the words rise to the ceiling. We sang to Heaven. Even though we had to get up early, Dad preached for nearly an hour, and we all prayed, one after the other. We asked God for clarity, for strength, for deliverance.

Rain pelted the earth outside when Dad woke us up. The thick, overcast sky was beginning to lighten up to the East, gray meeting black just above the line of rooftops. I saw that Mom was on her knees. I knew she had been awake for at least a few hours. Before our family stepped out across the stream that was spilling down the road, we all held hands and prayed one more time.

From outside the wall, the U.S. Embassy looked like a cage: crossed metal jutted to a point at the corners. It felt taller than its three stories. But it shone like a pearl against the dreary blanket over Nairobi.

After passing security, we were greeted by a smiling Kenyan, our translator, and a no-nonsense American who was all business under his closely cropped hairdo. I felt the cold of his blue eyes when they looked me up and down.

Dad went into the meeting room first. He emerged two hours later—the longest two hours of my life—shaking his head. "I don't know." Dad's voice was flat, his face expressionless. "Only God knows." I started to feel nervous. Mom was supposed to be called next, but after half an hour went by, the American said that there was no need to talk to her. He ushered our entire family inside.

While the Kenyan relayed his questions in a soothing voice, taking time to clearly form his words, the American watched, eyes, lips, and jaw carved against stone. It started simple enough—asking us our names and ages. Then, it felt like we were being tricked. The American would press my youngest sisters, repeating, "Are these your parents?" "Are these your brothers?" He never took his eyes off them when the girls spoke. The American repeated his questions, waiting to see if the girls were looking to my parents or us older kids for answers. It was as if he couldn't believe we were all one family.

I thought we had been trapped in there for hours, but only ten minutes had ticked by. On our way out, we were told that it would take three to four weeks for the results. As Mom herded the girls out the door she said, just loud enough for all of us to hear, "We did our best. Now, God, do your best."

I remember when Dad came home with our envelope. He acted like it had been any other day. Me and my brothers knew that he had just received a call from the Embassy, not more than an hour ago. But Dad held his empty hands out, telling us he was just out walking. I searched his face for even a hint of a smile. Nothing.

The Embassy does not let you past its iron gate when your decision is delivered. Too many people faint, or panic, or lose their minds, so the representatives at the Embassy don't tell you your results; they just slip you the envelope through a window and send you on your way to unpack what's inside. Dad told us the trick to knowing, though, even before you opened your letter. A heavy envelope means approval, light means rejection.

After Dad was done toying with us, he slapped a thick envelope on the table, unleashing the smile he had been holding back. "The angel has won the battle for us," he declared. Dad told us that the moment his fingers handled the envelope, he knew. Sure enough, there were orientation papers, medical forms—a pile of documents—accompanying our letter. Approved.

With the weight in his hand, Dad immediately felt a heavy burden lift from his shoulders—for the first time in years, he felt free. He was free. We all were.

I was so overwhelmed that I couldn't stand still, I couldn't bear to be enclosed. I ran outside, singing as loud as I could through the heaves and sobs. I danced in the streets, the girls chasing after me. John leapt in the air, kicking the sky.

We knew it was a miracle, nine years in the making.

It took six months to get through all of the orientation and required medical exams. Each one brought its own anxiety—the sting of the needle for a tuberculin skin test, followed by two days of watching the site and praying it didn't flare up, indicate an exposure to the bacteria. One failed test and it was game over.

And we had to be available at a moment's notice for our checkups. I remember the day we boarded the bus for our final medical exams. Our case had been idle for two months. I had been overcome, once again, by doubt. In my seat, I was anxious—I bounced my knees, ready to be at the clinic before the bus doors even shut.

But when I watched the city crawl past me out the window, everything felt wrong. The bus was going the wrong way. Soon, we were speeding. A man in the back yelled, waving a pistol. Another man, wearing plain street clothes, stood up in the middle of the bus, drawing a gun from his belt. I looked up front and saw that the conductor was also armed. His eyes never left the aisle as he talked with the driver, who was clearly in on it. We were being hijacked.

I wasn't even worried about what the men might take from my parents as the two thugs in the middle and back started robbing the passengers, one-by-one, shoving a barrel in the face of anyone who hesitated. I was more worried that if we missed our appointment that we would be stuck in Kenya.

The air was sucked out of the vehicle. I could hardly breathe. The men were not nervous at all; they went about their business like professionals, calm and composed. But they kept waving their guns to make sure everyone else remained on edge.

I kept thinking, *What a waste*. My family had sacrificed nine years, fighting starvation again and again, only for it to rest on the weight of a finger on a trigger. I thought about our angel and wondered if it was still fighting for us.

Suddenly, my body swung forward and slammed back against my seat as our bus skidded to a halt.

"The family," the conductor barked. "Get out." Three black pistols were trained on the other hostages as all eleven of us filed out of the bus. Dad exited last. His second foot had not even hit the ground when the driver floored it, speeding off in a cloud of dust with black treads scarring the pavement. My heart was too afraid to beat. Somehow, my feet managed to follow after my parents, who wasted no time in gathering their bearings to make our way to the hospital. It was a forty-five-minute walk, but we made it.

Of all the refugee families I knew—the ones who escaped the Congo with us, the ones from other countries in our community who were trying, like us, to get out of Kenya—ours was the first family granted a visa. Our friends surrounded us in celebration after we were cleared for departure. Even the ones who doubted us. After our voices were too tired to talk, our feet too weak to dance, and our eyes too heavy to stay open, Dad left them with one final message. It wasn't his usual long-winded sermon, but it rang just as true. "What is impossible with man is possible with God" Luke 18:27 (ESV).

///

On July 14, 2009, I held my breath as I climbed up a blinding white staircase leading up into the plane. The sound of metal clinging off the wheels of the other passengers' luggage was music to my ears. Behind me, the afternoon sun rippled off the curved glass edge of Jomo Kenyatta International Airport.

Mom had Esther pressed tightly against her chest. My sister had woken me up several times in the night with violent coughs. It was just a bad cold, but I was nervous that security might prevent us from boarding the plane. One cough could undo everything, I feared. I didn't bother looking back out at Kenya as I stepped through the curtain of shadow and into the artificial light of the airplane's passenger tunnel. I'd said my goodbye to the city at the terminal gate. That was enough for me.

I kept my ear trained on Esther. I was waiting for that explosive sound, for security to emerge in their crisp, light blue shirts to take us away. But she did not make a sound. I exhaled a flood of wind, praising God through the heavy sigh.

In Kenya, as a refugee boy with nothing, I had promised to serve God with my life. I also wrestled with doubts that I would have much of a life to serve Him with. I feared that if God did not deliver us that we would die in Kenya as refugees. Sinking into the plush seat, clicking a seatbelt tight around my waist, God reminded me that He was the one in control. I only had to follow.

As the plane rattled and bounded up the tarmac, I watched my old life blaze by—war and hunger, fear and disappointment, sacrifice and heartache flickered and blurred out, like the sunlight over the Kenyan horizon out the window. My body grew lighter as I soared higher and higher.

It was the greatest feeling of my life.

Chapter Eleven

The Ntiboneras Arrive
2009-2012

M y fingers glided across the electric keyboard. The sensation was calming. As I sunk deep into my thoughts, searching for words to express my gratitude to God for all He brought me through, my hands teased out melodies. I'd stop, play back a few notes, and then scribble some words on paper, the ink crying out from the depths of my heart.

Seven thousand, seven hundred and thirty-six miles separated me from Nairobi, from the hunger and desolation. Twenty-two hours had taken me from Kenya to Brussels and then over the rippling blue Atlantic to New York City. From the air I had watched a dense jungle of industry rise up, tearing through the clouds. It made Nairobi seem like a village. I felt like I was on a different planet. Thin as a needle, I found myself in a land of giants when I stepped off the plane into the crowded terminal. At least that's how all the people appeared in my mind. There wasn't much of a view out the airport window, but just the sight of a smooth, six-lane road took my breath away. I'd never seen anything like it before. After a few hours, with night starting to put out the flaming horizon, I was in the air again, headed for Greensboro, North Carolina—our new home. My home.

Behind me, seven thousand, seven hundred and thirty-six miles and an ocean of time expanding by the second.

Not long after Lutheran Family Services settled my family into a three-bedroom apartment in Greensboro, I was given the keyboard. The present was life-changing.

John received a guitar, and we were also gifted with songbooks. As unfamiliar as my new world was, music brought a sense of familiarity to our household. It was the one thing I carried with me from Africa to the United States. The song in my heart could not be stopped by borders, mountains, or seas. Music was what brought my parents together. I inherited it from them. As a refugee, music helped me forget about my place in the world. I would lose myself in the sound, the notes rattling in my bones, strengthening them. The harmonies and melodies soothed the hunger pains.

No matter how difficult my circumstances were, music was my oasis; I could always reach it.

But I had never played an instrument before I got my keyboard. The black and white keys unlocked a new form of expression for me as I taught myself to play. My fingers would dance a melody as I put notes to the words I'd written on paper. I would stop, change keys, and play again, until I got the sound just right, to match what was in my head.

John and I each learned to play on our own, spending many sleepless nights playing along to YouTube videos. Our living room was constantly filled with harmonies as my siblings sang together, often rumbling the floor with dancing feet.

Outside, I was adapting slowly, like a snake warming itself on a rock after a cold night. Everyone talked so fast that I couldn't catch all the words. They whipped past my ears like the cars on the freeway. And my tongue felt like it was stuck in mud whenever I spoke. I was insecure about my accent at first. As my English improved—partly because of the school for refugees and immigrants that prepared me to go on and earn my high school diploma at a community college—I grew to embrace my accent. It's a part of who I am, a reminder of the life I've lived, what I've left behind, and what I've overcome.

Even though our needs were always met, life was hard to adjust to in its own way. I remember stepping onto the polished tile of our new kitchen and pulling open the cupboards. They were stocked full of food. For a refugee, it was a dream come true. But I didn't have an appetite.

When I was soaring over the ocean, I fantasized about how I was going to eat and eat, never stopping, filling my stomach like never before. For a few days, however, I could barely hold down more than a few bites. My first meal in the new place was a boxed dinner—chicken and rice with broccoli. I'd never had broccoli before. Chicken and rice were familiar enough, until I bit into it. The taste was unfamiliar. I wasn't disappointed or upset, my mouth just couldn't recognize what it was chewing. It took a while to get used to the flavors. Beans especially. My first bite of beans was so sweet that I almost spit them out—the sugar was overwhelming.

But my appetite returned as I buried years of starvation in a pile of new flavors—crunchy, salted pretzels, spicy burritos, pasta with tangy red sauce, the rich, oily, juicy sensation of biting into a Chick-fil-A sandwich. The first time my teeth snapped a stalk of asparagus, filling my mouth with the strong, slightly bitter flavor, I was hooked.

I got my first real job at an American grill-style restaurant. The mouth-watering smell of sizzling beef soaked the air. I was eager to serve food, but all the orders buzzed around my head like bugs in the jungle. So, they kept me in the back. I still felt a real sense of accomplishment, scrubbing grime down the drain, suds popping off my arms while I polished dishes until they sparkled. I was independent, earning something on my own. Taking out the garbage was an eye-opener, however. I still can't get over how much perfectly good food was tied up in plastic bags and set out to rot in a rusty metal box outside. The refugee boy inside me wanted to scream.

So much of what is considered normal in America was new to me. I don't think most Americans realize how blessed they are. I remember I would see all these teenagers driving cars. You could walk by a high school and see a parking lot full of cars—red ones, blue ones, black, yellow, silver, green—every color you could imagine. Back in Africa, even a university parking lot didn't have as many cars. You could count them. Having a car was a sign of prosperity where I had come from.

Even after coming home damp and sore from washing dishes, the smell of hamburger weighing heavy on my shirt, I wouldn't be able to still my mind enough to close my eyes until I played out a few lines of music. Many times, a song or two turned into an entire night of practice, my eyes burning through the exhaustion as my hands fought to master the keyboard.

Music eased the culture shock. I spent all of my free time, many long nights, tracing patterns across the keys of my new instrument, uncovering familiar chords. And I wrote new songs.

Many times, flipping the feather-light pages of my Bible would spark inspiration. I'd set my pen to paper and use the ink to pour out my heart to God. Songwriting helped me process my past and channel it into praise.

I also wrote with John, who would pluck strings on his guitar while we bounced words back and forth. Or I would sit down on the couch with Priscilla, stitching poetry together out of the frayed threads pulled from our shared experiences.

Our family time of prayer and worship has always been filled with music. This has helped tighten the inseparable bond within our family. In America, those past cries of desperation were replaced with shouts of joy as our voices blended with the instruments, ringing louder and clearer than ever inside those plastered walls.

Whenever there was an argument in our household, John or Asi would pick up a guitar and start strumming gently, or I would tap out a soft melody on the keys. From the other side of the room, one of the girl's voices would rise up, joined quickly by Mom's. One by one, our voices would roll in until we were all singing, harmony flooding the house from floor to ceiling, washing away the heated emotions.

Music also became a way for us to tell our story.

After living in the U.S. for about one year, my brothers and I had outgrown our former group name, The Congo Boys, and became The Ntiboneras. My sisters were as much a part of my family's story as any of us, so they danced alongside us on the stage.

Our first public performance was at a refugee festival in downtown Greensboro. In brightly-colored tank-tops, me and my siblings—all ten of us—danced in unison, traditional grass skirts spraying from our hips, slapping our thighs, as our bare feet pounded the stage. Beads rattled around our necks. We kicked our feet and clapped our hands high above our heads as Baraka and Christian beat a fast rhythm on their drums. Swahili verses rolled off our tongues. Adili and Naomi's braids danced along with us in the wind—the other girls had their hair in tight cornrows. For the audience, it was a cultural experience; for us, it was a way to express our heritage and to begin to share all God had done for us in bringing us to the States.

We kept performing. Our story spread, without us even having to search for gigs. The Greensboro Children's Museum hosted us. Churches started inviting us, one by one. We'd dance barefoot on the soft, red carpet of a Methodist church one week and the hardwood floor on a Pentecostal stage the next.

By the time I was two years into my studies at Liberty University in Virginia, my family band had been invited all the way to St. Louis to perform over Christmas break. We packed our gear into a rental van and drove across the wide, open interstates. The trip was almost as far as when we had ridden from Bukavu to Nairobi.

One day, as my family's music was just blossoming, Dad presented a gift to me and my siblings. In my hands, he set his notebook. I traced the lines in the dark, worn leather. I could feel the years roll back as I opened the journal, time written in the creases of its cover. The book was older than me by at least a decade. Inside, the yellowing pages displayed Dad's handwriting. Unlike my own hurried script, Dad had drawn each letter with precision. His words were like works of art. I strained reading words. Everything was in Mashi, my parent's tribal tongue—Dad has had to help me translate it. I spoke it as a kid, but reading it is still a challenge. To this day I write songs in that book. And my own writing has come to imitate Dad's careful, artistic style. I've had him help me write a song in Mashi, fusing his words with mine.

Although writing helped me to begin to process my story, I still had not fully embraced who I was. I needed to set out on my own, to discover where God was taking me. But I had no idea then that I would be pulled back to where He had first brought me into this world.

Chapter Twelve

Looking Back
2013-2015

When I moved to Virginia to go to Liberty University, it was hard to be away from my parents, brothers, and sisters. It was the first time in my life when I was on my own. I know many people experience these types of feelings when they go away to college—I missed my mom's cooking, being able to walk down the hall and find John or Baraka if I needed to talk—but after all we survived together, I had come to depend on them, and they on me.

There were prayer meetings I could attend at school, although not every night. Sometimes, I would find myself sitting alone on my bed in my dorm room feeling the weight of my family's absence—no hands to hold for prayer. I'd put on my headphones to fill the emptiness with music. Even though the songs were American—contemporary worship—I could still sing praises under my breath and feel that special bond, built in Africa, and the strength that brought us through the fire of struggle, warming my chest. Even though I missed my family, I was constantly reminded about why I had chosen this Christian college.

Liberty University is like no place on earth. You can feel the spirit of the Lord alive on campus—in the people, in the atmosphere. It's a little slice of Heaven. I learned about Liberty while searching for colleges online. As I read more about its mission—to train world changers in every profession to impact every corner of the globe for Christ—I knew that it was a place where I could grow in my faith as well as receive a good education.

At the time, I wanted to be a doctor. The night Mom nearly died after giving birth to Esther haunted me; I could still see the blood soaked into Dad's shirt when he came home. I wanted to play my part in making sure no one else would have to endure what my parents went through that night. I wanted to save lives. More than that, I wanted to bring change to the healthcare system in the Congo. So, I went to Liberty and majored in health promotion.

The campus was beautiful. I remember the first time I saw it when I visited for a college weekend experience. In the distance, the horizon rolled like waves, a deep blue over the sunset, where God painted the sky with soft pinks, rich purples, and fire orange. They were baby mountains compared to the ones in my motherland. But they were still breathtaking.

At university, I made friends with my feet. Pickup soccer games on the neatly trimmed grass was the perfect place to meet people. It didn't matter where you came from—or that I had learned the game on uneven dirt roads kicking plastic bags—all that mattered was having fun. When rain soaked the field to a sticky swamp, or if it was so cold that it hurt to breathe, we could play inside, under the high metal roof of the massive indoor soccer center. Whether I was chasing a ball in the open air, with the baby mountains in the distance, or bouncing passes off the high plastic walls of one of the twin bright green turf sheets, I could connect with people. Soccer was a way to relate to others.

I experienced the fullness of God's kingdom as I made friends with people from all around the world; people from many different states, and countries like Brazil, Korea, and even African neighbors from Uganda, Rwanda—people I would have actually had less of a chance to meet living in my motherland.

After a semester at Liberty, I convinced John and Baraka to join me. We moved into a small apartment together where we wrote songs when we weren't out playing soccer or doing homework. It was hard to concentrate on my schoolwork sometimes. Writing was the hardest part; I had to translate my thoughts from Swahili into English and then write them down. It was double the work.

One of the most extraordinary things about Liberty is its regular Convocation services. Thousands of students gather in a large arena under a domed roof for worship. The voices blend together as one, praising God. When I walked in the room, I could feel the electricity running through my body, the beat of the drums pounding with my heart, guitars ringing between my ribs. The music was led by a band of students, the Liberty Worship Collective. But we often had special guest musicians to lead worship, including Chris Tomlin, Elevation, Hillsong, Jesus Culture. Liberty is an exciting place that attracts exciting people.

I never missed a Convo. The gathering, which took place on Mondays, Wednesdays, and Fridays when I was there, is not actually a chapel service, even though many great preachers came to speak. The mission of Convo is to challenge students spiritually and intellectually, so we also heard from athletes, movie stars, politicians, and other leaders in culture.

I liked to stand in the back with a clear view of the entire room, an enormous bowl where the faces would light up in bright colors as special lights panned the stands. We sang our hearts out to God. My ears devoured the sweet harmony rising from the floor.

The routine of college was comforting—absorbing data in class on how to stop epidemics from spreading or how fat is broken down and turned into energy before burning off my own on the grass with John at my side and Baraka dancing with the soccer ball between his feet ahead. Or feeling the strain of metal fighting my muscles behind the expansive glass gym wall, grabbing a chicken sandwich, and then trying to keep my eyes open at my desk as words crawled from my fingers to the blinding white screen. I'd wake up in the morning and find myself refreshed with a shower of worship at another uplifting Convo.

But then, one day, with the sturdy weight of the desk chair beneath me, I would still feel off balance. The chair was comfortable. *I* was comfortable. But for some reason, it felt wrong. I was reminded of the cold, hard floor in Nairobi. Or, in my bed, I would wake up tangled in my sheets, legs stretched out on my mattress. I had so much room that it was strangely suffocating. I remembered being piled on top of my brothers in our tiny room in Kenya fighting off pangs of hunger. It wasn't that I missed the old sensations—especially as I piled chicken on my plate at the dining hall, a dozen scents competing for my appetite: burgers, pizza, fried rice, tacos, pasta, whatever I wanted—I just had a nagging feeling in my gut that I didn't quite understand. God was speaking to me. I sensed Him, I was listening, I just hadn't heard His voice clearly yet.

In Convo, I would hear about amazing projects taking place all over the world. Everyone went crazy when Tim Tebow came—there were girls packing the front row, wearing football jerseys and waving posters that sparkled with glitter. I remember Tebow talked about how he was building a hospital for kids in the Philippines. The giant scoreboard played a video of him lifting small children up on his large shoulders. I pictured the kids as Congolese.

Another time, as Bob Goff yelled and waved his arms all across the stage, he told a story about how he decided to step out of his comfort zone and help hurting people in Uganda. Inside, my heart raced. *That's less than a day's drive from the Congo!*

When I heard about my classmates spending their spring break in Spain, ministering to North African refugees, I felt myself shrink back to a boy, a dirty shirt hanging from my bony shoulders. I wondered who was coming for me, for the children who still lived the life I once had.

During another Convo, I leaned over to John, wrapped in the dark of the auditorium, and whispered, "One day the Congo is going to be mentioned on that stage." He nodded. We started praying, with Baraka joining, too. We asked the Lord that everyone at Liberty would hear about the Democratic Republic of the Congo. Just like when I was asking for shoes over my bare feet, I didn't realize that as I was praying, God was preparing me to be the answer to that prayer.

I started to realize, in the comfort of my desk chair or while going back for a second plate in the dining hall, how far I had come. I would look over my shoulder when I walked to class, past the monstrous brick buildings and towering white columns, and see an empty muddy street. The comfort of my rubber soles reminded me of how the dirt used to grind into the cracks in my toes, how rocks stabbed my heels. I had grown comfortable in the States—too comfortable. I had spent so much time running away from my life of hardship that I did not realize I was still coasting forward, even though there was no longer anything to run from.

I talked to my parents on the phone almost every night. After hanging up, I would toss my phone to the side and let my head sink into my pillow. Dad's voice would stay with me. Behind my eyes, I could still hear him talking over the rhythm of footsteps while an endless mob of faces tangled around me. My heart raced as the bodies pushed in from all sides overhead. I heard the kids screaming. Dad's voice rumbled over the noise, "Keep moving forward; don't look back." My feet stepped in time. I knew that it was important to keep pressing on. Everyone around us drummed to the same beat, over and over. *Don't look back.* It was a matter of life or death.

On my bed, with the mattress bending to support my weight, I could hear God telling me, *It's OK. It's time to look back now.*

I told my brothers how I was feeling and that we were too relaxed here. So, together, in late 2014, we started a nonprofit organization. We wanted to use the blessings we had been given to make a difference in our motherland. Our name—Ntibonera—means, "surprise in a good way." John suggested that we use the family name for the foundation. He wanted to surprise the African people who felt overlooked by giving them hope, reminding them they are not forgotten and to not give up. We were blessed by so many friends—many of them from our Greensboro church, Hope Chapel—who helped us to get the Ntibonera Foundation running.

Around the same time, my parents began to reconnect with people from the Congo online.

In 2015, I learned that my cousin, Safari Ludwakali—I call him "uncle"—was in danger. Rebels kicked down his door one night and took everything that he owned. When they stormed the house, the rebels unloaded a stream of bullets into his son, Rick. I could only remember Rick's seven-year-old face—always smiling. He was a strong boy, short and built like a truck. Though he was younger than me, he could almost outrun me and had no trouble wrestling me to the ground. Rick could never stay still, he was always active, always playing. He was only 19 when he died in a pool of blood on his own bed.

After killing my cousin and leaving with armfuls of his possessions, the men threatened Uncle Safari, telling him they were coming back to kill everyone else.

It was hard for me to picture my uncle terrified, as I knew he was. In my head, he was still a wiry tree growing out of thick, black combat boots, looking down at me. His eyes glowed like the blade of his machete as he warned me and John to protect ourselves all those years ago. It hurt me to learn what Uncle Safari went through.

Mom and Dad sent him money so that he could escape and settle in a refugee camp in Uganda.

In my closet, I ran my fingers across my clothes. Sleeves brushed my hand, one-by-one, like leaves in the endless jungle. A thought had been nagging at me since a Convocation a few weeks earlier where I looked down at the floor and saw all the different shoes. Boots, sneakers, slides, heels—like fish in the sea there were so many patterns, shapes, and sizes. I had never felt the ground in Virginia. On the floor of the closet, I found shoes that I didn't even wear anymore.

I remembered the smell of smoke lingering on my shirt in Kenya: a tangy sensation in my nostrils. At night, I would take off my clothes and soak them in a bucket. My hands throbbed after sliding the clothes up and down against the bumpy wooden board, water splashing up my arms while scrubbing my outfit clean. I would have to hang my clothes outside, as close to the fire as possible so they would be dry for me to wear to church the next day.

In the States, I could pile up a week's worth of laundry and still have options. And I knew all of my friends could, too. I started noticing how often a bright red T-shirt or wild striped pattern would reappear on one of my friends. I saw how blessed I was to live like I did—how blessed we all were.

It was in response to this realization, God pulling a thread in my heart, when I flipped open a brown, cardboard box and filled it up with shoes and clothes. I had no idea what this simple act would grow into; I was just following a tug from God. But ever since that day, I have continued to collect unwanted clothes and shoes. I remembered what I had needed as a refugee. I couldn't let those good items go to waste.

I spread my message across America as The Ntiboneras continued to travel, performing at churches, conferences, and other events: all of us in America have so many things that we take for granted, so much of it collecting dust in our closets, let's put them to good use in the hands of those who need them.

The boxes were just starting to burst out of my closet when I started contemplating a return trip to the Congo. I felt desperate to go back home. It had been fifteen years since I had stepped foot in my motherland, and I knew that there was at least one relative I would never see again. Since there was not enough time for me to plan the logistics to ship the clothes and shoes I had collected overseas, I had to leave most of it behind. That was disappointing, but my vision for what to do with the stuff was not fully clear, anyway. I would soon learn why God sent me ahead to the Congo. He wanted to open my eyes.

Chapter Thirteen

Fresh Wounds
(Homecoming Part II)
2015

The ball in my stomach expanded as the Congo drew closer. Fifteen years, a lifetime to a college student like myself, had passed since I had last been held in the arms of my motherland. I was excited, heart skipping, as I watched Africa rise beneath my feet. My imagination ran as wild as an elephant in Virunga National Park. I pictured how things would have improved for my people—wider, paved streets with traffic lights, electricity glowing out of homes at night, fresh, white hospitals with open beds and near-empty waiting rooms. Still, unease rolled around inside me. I couldn't identify it, exactly. And the anticipation held it down.

Having my dad and two of my brothers—John and Baraka—by my side was comforting. Seeing their familiar faces, faces that had been with me almost as long as I could remember (longer, in Dad's case) eased the strain in my gut.

As we rolled through Rwanda, straight for the Congo after landing at Kamembe International Airport, I found myself lost between time. I was winding back, retracing my steps toward the motherland I had left behind. But my eyes also saw a vision of the future—Congo's future. The Rwandan infrastructure looked solid. As we were gliding across slick pavement, I saw yellow and tan faces of homes smiling at me from under red caps. In the sturdy foundations of buildings rising out of the green landscape, in the unscarred dips and bends of tar and asphalt on the road ahead, in the casual steps of people crossing the marketplace, I saw a country that had started healing its wounds. It did not feel like the same country I had cut across all those years ago.

Rwanda is a miracle. After the horrors it endured in the '90s, today it is one of the cleanest and safest countries in Africa. Incredible.

I remember how the ache inside faded in the back of my taxi. Instead, I felt a small flutter of hope glide in circles: *Maybe Congo will be just like this.* Anticipation brought me all the way to the international bridge before the weight crashed down on me. The bridge was straight, even. But I felt like the empty-bellied kid climbing uphill, a load of bricks crushing down on my head.

Just breathing in Congolese air was different. It wasn't as simple to identify as pollution or smoke—but there was a sense that what was coming in was soiled, dirty. The air was heavier. I was reminded that there was a reason my family had left the Congo. When I heard birds cawing in the distance, I flinched, half expecting to hear guns.

Disappointed, I rode deeper into Bukavu. It wasn't as reckless as running back into a burning building—the war had been over for years—but I felt like I was heading through the charred aftermath of a blaze. I didn't even recognize my own country anymore.

I had to look harder. My eyes traced the rise of the peaks in the distance, slipped down a slope of roofs pointing upward through green curtains, and followed the edge of the city as it dug its fingers into the bottom of the greyish waters. The rolls and curves, shapes and textures, were all familiar. I was looking into a face that had aged overnight.

When Grandpa Ntibonera appeared to greet me, I saw the years written on his face—I hadn't seen him since I was a boy, younger than ten. But I knew his long jaw, salted with facial hair trimmed under high, hard cheekbones. I recognized the glimmer in his bright brown eyes, even as they had glazed. And even as water drowned them out. Tears rolled down my face, too, as we embraced. My arms squeezed him in like a python around a tree. Even though I outweighed him, I felt power in his embrace, a body that fought the strain of village farming every day of his life.

I didn't even notice that I was surrounded by family. All this time, I had no idea who had survived, and my extended family had been as uncertain of my fate. I kept wiping my eyes, drying my cheeks, as I went from aunt to uncle to cousin to aunt, hugging bodies weathered by hardship, but alive and well. I had to introduce myself to many more unfamiliar faces, cousins who were born and had grown like weeds in my absence. So much had changed. The reunion swelled over three days to seventy or eighty people. All day we hugged and reminisced, talking through mouthfuls of chicken and rice, dancing around drums in the street, until the moon was tired and the flickers from lamps lighting the windows along the street had each gone out.

I spent time on my own, wandering the streets of my childhood. Around me, the city was overrun, overpopulated, and run down. Buildings were crumbling into filthy, dusty roads. The only tarmac I saw was a stretch that cut through neatly trimmed grass and rows of trees from the governor's house to the main road.

What was left of the field where I once played soccer was a small wasteland, empty and lifeless in the shadow of rows and rows of shacks.

Talking with the people who appeared out of ramshackle homes propped up against the sturdy, stone-and-brick walls, I learned that rebels continued to attack villages. The people were helpless—like the rabbits in my grandpa's pen when the jungle cat broke in. Villagers flocked to the city for safety, leaving behind everything they knew.

My childhood neighborhood was suffocating; I couldn't even find the house where I used to live. As I searched, I started to play back memories. It helped push back the rusty tin walls closing in. There were trails of small footprints pressed in the dirt and, in my mind, I saw me and John running after a pack of our friends, adding more marks in the road. The rattle of pots over cooking stoves stirred a rhythm inside me. I looked for the clearings where us boys would practice our dance routines.

Lost in joyful memories, I bumped into two strangers. The men were about my age. Their faces lit up when they saw me, white teeth spreading big smiles across their faces as they started talking so fast that my ears couldn't keep up. I didn't recognize them any more than the neighborhood around me. As I looked closer, however, I noticed how one of them, who was bald, favored his left hand and that his bottom teeth jutted out. The other man's left eye squinted. A flash of light exploded in my memory—Pascale and Kabgi, my childhood friends. They were all grown up, but their telling features peeled back the disguise of age. I grabbed them and hugged them tightly. I thought they had died during the war.

Pascale had a scar running across his shaved head. As his fingers traced the line across his scalp, he told me how he had been shot in the head. A stray bullet caught him while he was running from an attack in a crowd. With blood pouring from the wound, he tried to keep on going. But his vision blurred, and his legs buckled under him. Pascale laid on the ground, blood everywhere, trying to get up. He watched the world above him spin until blackness punched him to sleep. Then, he woke up and found himself in the hospital. Miraculously, he survived.

I was overwhelmed with emotion when I heard Pascale's story. "Man, God is good!" The words slipped out with my tears. I could not believe I was standing there with him, after all those years.

We walked together, the three of us, remembering all the things we did together as kids. Pascale was my best friend growing up; he was always right there by my side dancing in the street concerts. Or weaving ahead of me with John, finding an opening for me to place a pass on the soccer field. I remembered how he would make me talk to girls with him; I was shy, blushing as he dragged me over to a group of pretty faces.

As we talked, it stung me deep inside—the feeling where my childhood had been ripped away.

Traffic in Bukavu was chaos. There were no rules in place, and nobody obeyed them anyway. Intersections jammed while vehicles plowed through crowds of people with barely enough room to get out of the way. Horns roared at each other until one car would back away so the other could squeeze past.

Public transportation was like riding a tree trunk down a cliff in the jungle. You crammed inside the metal box—on one taxi ride I was with seven others in a small sedan, four people in front and four in the back—and then you rattled your way over the uneven ground until you crashed through enough obstacles to come to a stop, hopefully your destination. One time I rode in a van and the driver had Baraka sit on a stool leaning against the dash. He had taken the seat out so more people could squeeze inside.

Corruption was rampant. Traffic police would stop me to ask for money. I had to carry extra bills wherever I went to avoid the hassle of being shaken down. People walked by, unaffected. To them, power existed to be abused.

My people dragged through the streets with heavy eyes. After rape, murder, and hunger had become so widespread that it was normal, they had learned to live through fear and uncertainty without hiding inside every time rumors heated up. With locked, rigid shoulders, they went about their business, carrying on with the invisible burden. They were tired from war, in search of peace. And they were looking for leaders who would care for them. Now that the war was over, corruption and poor leadership had calloused the people's hopes.

I noticed the familiar sunken gaze, skin pulled tight over cheeks from missed meals, all around me.

I wanted to reach out. I could feel their pain—I'd lived that life, the life of fear, desperation, and hunger. I knew God saved my life and that he could do that and more for these people. God was telling me I needed to fight for them, since their leaders wouldn't.

People were struggling just to get a dollar. After church one Sunday, I stayed outside the heavy wooden doors to greet the people as they left. An old woman stared at me from across the street. I watched her out of the corner of my eye as a field of floral head wraps paraded by me, women smiling and hugging me. The scrawny woman just stood there, face as unreadable as a tree. I was struck by her. I pushed through the congregation and walked over to her. I pulled five dollars out of my pocket—everything I had with me—and set the folded bills in her small, wrinkled hand. This old woman broke out dancing, right there in the street. She had to be at least seventy. Her feet talked like a schoolgirl, however, fast as a whip, all over the place. "God bless you my son," her voice rose above the cross atop the church, "you and your generation." I learned that the woman had not had a meal for three days.

Even though it was nice to interact with people in the city, I also had work to do. My foundation had assembled a coalition of Congolese pastors through some of my Dad's old ministry contacts and we spent time meeting and planning ways to restore hope in our people.

Since people were flooding the city from the villages, I knew that I would have to start at the source: the deep, green sea of trees. I was going to reach out to the neglected people to tell them they were not forgotten.

Under a canopy of gray cloud, I set off in a rented truck for Chibuga, a village of Pygmies buried far in the jungle.

There are more than six-hundred thousand[12] Pygmies in the Congo. Not a one is more than five feet tall. Baraka had researched about their struggles and recommended that our organization make an effort to connect with them. These villagers were once hunters and gatherers in the forest. They were a proud people who found sustenance and medicine from the thick, wooded areas they called home. But one day, the government decided that it had better use for their land and kicked them out, relocating them to a smaller plot. Because of the cramped space, the Pygmies were not able to cultivate land to farm—skills they didn't have anyway because farming was not necessary to their past way of life. Their new land also had no access to clean water or medical aid.

Pygmies desire to be accepted by society and live like everyone else, but they feel like outcasts. People often treat them as if they are less than human. They are told their size is a deformity, something to be ashamed of. So, they run away from strangers, hiding for fear of being laughed at or viewed like animals.

I knew that the people of Chibuga and those like them suffered from extreme poverty. I decided that I was not going to go out to the villages with only a Bible in my hands. Christ's words in Matthew 25:34-40 (NIV) were a key passage of inspiration for my foundation:

> *Then the King will say to those on His right, 'Come, you who are blessed by my Father; take your inheritance, the kingdom prepared for you since the creation of the world. For I was hungry and you gave me something to eat, I was thirsty and you gave me something to drink, I was a stranger and you invited me in, I needed clothes and you clothed me, I was sick and you looked after me, I was in prison and you came to visit me.'*
>
> *Then the righteous will answer Him, 'Lord, when did we see you hungry and feed you, or thirsty and give you something to drink? When did we see you a stranger and invite you in, or needing clothes and clothe you? When did we see you sick or in prison and go to visit you?'*
>
> *The King will reply, 'Truly I tell you, whatever you did for one of the least of these brothers and sisters of mine, you did for me.'*

I did not expect someone who had not had a meal for three, four, or five days to listen to me preach Jesus' hope and believe what I was teaching them. People could collapse and die in my arms while I spoke. Since we live in this world, with all of its brokenness, as Christians I believe we have a responsibility to those who are in need. Feeding the needy, serving one another, is a way of serving Christ.

Even though I hadn't brought the shoe donations with me on this trip, I did not go into the villages empty handed. Using as much of my savings as I could spare, I purchased ten bags of rice and beans, as well as some salt and candies. I loaded those on a truck with the apparel I was able to bring. Liberty's Intramural Sports Department gave me three hundred jackets and two hundred T-shirts to distribute. These were nice items, just with outdated logos. Some friends and family were disappointed that I didn't bring them a jacket, but I had to tell them those gifts had a purpose: I was only giving them to people in need.

When our transport crashed through the thick wall of brush and leaves into Chibuga, I was hit in the face with desolation beyond anything I had experienced.

I was surrounded by small mud huts, mops of grass for roofs. I could see how the rains would get in and soak the ground inside. When the sun was out, it baked the people inside their homes like ovens. They were hardly protected.

Children were running around barefoot, infections eating away their feet. Everywhere I looked, jiggers rotted flesh. I didn't see one pair of shoes. It broke my heart. I had no idea that children were still battling these soil-transmitted infections, so easily preventable. I was told that the village children couldn't go to school and adults couldn't go to work because it was too painful to walk very far. *How could this still exist in the Congo?*

I was crying in my heart, remembering the boxes of shoes in my closet. It felt so inadequate that I had only brought some food and clothes, and not enough to go around.

No one would come near me at first. Kids would creep close, poking their heads through a tuft of tall grass and then run and hide when I turned toward them. I pulled out a fistful of Twizzlers, fanning the red chords at the crouching kids. With wide eyes, they emerged. Once one of the tiny kids took a cautious bite, then devoured the sweet rope in an instant, the other children mobbed us. Below me, outstretched hands flooded my field of vision. I watched joy erupt on their faces as they tore into the sweets. I felt so blessed to be able to bring them that small taste of luxury. The gift opened a door so that I could start to talk to them, to spend time with them and show them that they were valued.

When Dad started to preach, the trees were the only things moving. Branches swayed silent while the Pygmies listened to him explain that we were friends and that we were not there to laugh at them. He said a friend doesn't mock another person in need; they help them. He wanted the villagers to realize they were not outcasts, that God in Heaven looks down on them with love, that Jesus, God's son, sacrificed himself so that they could be part of God's family. Dad told the people of Chibuga that we considered them to be our family.

We spent the rest of the day trying to break through their unease by talking to them and giving them food and clothes. Just as I feared, there wasn't enough for everyone. People would come up to me, holding up hands that had been chewed raw. I had no more food to offer. Frail bodies all around me looked like they would snap any moment. I just promised, over and over, to one shrunken, desperate face after the next, that I would come back, that I would bring more with me the next time. Honestly, I had no idea how I could help those people; my hands were empty. I didn't know what I was going to do—I'd given everything that I had brought with me. Still, I promised that I would be back.

As people opened up to me, they explained that men had come to the village before. They took advantage of them. People would come in, take their pictures, and then disappear forever, using the footage to advance their agendas or to attract donation money and supplies that never reached the Pygmies. The people vow to come back as they leave, but the words evaporate with the jungle mists. They don't come back. That was part of the reason the villagers were so isolated, so slow to trust outsiders. They didn't want to be used and discarded anymore.

I continued to sow promises, like seeds. But I wasn't throwing them to the wind—I was determined not to let those people down. The experience rooted deep in me. The scars of my own past, though they had healed, certainly left their mark on me. But this was different. Something within me snapped. I would never be the same.

Ten days came and went like waves washing up and pulling back away on the shore. When it was time for me to leave the Congo again, I was disappointed, but I carried the images from Chibuga with me in my mind. A new passion kindled within me. The burning fire was about to spread to my family and consume my foundation, shining a light for the people hidden in Congo's shadows.

When I got back to America, I got right to work. By God, I was going to keep my promise.

Chapter Fourteen
A House Full of Shoes
2015-2016

The electric hum from amplifiers would still be ringing in my ears when I began stuffing secondhand sneakers into boxes. A pair of shoes, new or gently used, was the entry fee for our concerts. After our performances, my family and I would pack them up in cardboard and squeeze them between our instrument cases in our car or rental van. On a good night, there wouldn't be much room left for all the bodies; we would put boxed shoes under our seats and in our laps.

From the day I returned to the States my family was on board with my mission. I didn't even sleep off the jet lag before I gathered everyone into the living room to tell them what God had placed on my heart.

It was going to be a lot of hard work, but my family was with me all the way.

We traveled as often as we could—I was driving a couple hours down to North Carolina from Liberty a few weekends every month and I did my best to fill up my breaks as much as possible.

The Ntiboneras drove all across North Carolina and travelled down to Atlanta, up to Delaware, and across the map to Kansas City and Minneapolis. Our family band would fill up the stage at smaller churches where our music stuffed the packed houses. We played in front of larger crowds, dozens, usually more than one hundred people at a time, under old, vaulted ceilings as people danced above in the balconies. The modern horseshoe auditoriums wrapped around us like lakes. Some of our events drew more than fifteen hundred people. When we left, it was like we were unloading an entire shoe factory.

Our music was a fusion of our diverse heritage. We liked to play contemporary worship songs, familiar spiritual anthems that people could sing along to. But you couldn't take the Africa out of us either. Our original music is a blend of rich flavors—pop hooks, seben rhythms, Kenyan vibes, even some traditional tribal influences. We still put our seben twist on familiar songs, spicing them up with fast, hard African beats, smooth baselines, and fluttering melodies. The concerts were wild celebrations to God.

After putting on such upbeat shows, we would soon find ourselves in dark, empty auditoriums with loads of shoes piled up by the stage. When we first started doing shoe drives, this was a bit of a shock. Our energy had been spent. Concerts are hard work. But we didn't think about who was going to pack up the shoes. Me and my siblings would load them up in our car with our gear. At home, Mom and Dad would sort and pack up the shoes during the week.

In the dead of winter, air biting like the wild dogs that roamed my Kenyan neighborhood, I got a call from a church telling me they had collected shoes for me. It was below freezing. To my African blood, it was torture. But I bundled up in my coat, wrapped a scarf around my neck and went out the door. When I got home, late into the night, Mom was waiting up. She came out into the freezing air to help. I told her to go back inside before she turned to ice, but she stayed up with me to help anyway.

I felt like my dream was becoming a burden for everyone in the house. I tried to lead by example. When we headed off to another gig, after just performing the entire weekend before, I would shake off the weight of my own fatigue and lead the way. I'd be the first to start loading up the car, the first to unload it at the church, and jump down off the stage as soon as the show was done and get the packing going.

They say two is better than one. Well, eleven is better than two. I am so thankful to each and every member of my family for what they meant to the shoe drive. I could see how tired they were, the way their feet dragged around the house when we weren't out performing. But they never complained and always kept a positive attitude. I could not have accomplished what I have in my life without each one of my family members.

Our hard work, sacrifice, and dedication brought in more footwear than we were prepared to handle. My entire life changed as I was on this mission. My time in undergrad passed by like all of the streetlights and signs blurring into streaks of red and gold outside our window while the van rolled down highways. I got my health promotion degree in 2016 and set right to work on a Master of Business Administration degree with Liberty. God had redirected my career, so I followed: to rural towns, suburbs, and big cities. Fortunately, I was able to take classes online so that I could continue to travel.

When I was a kid, the Congo was my entire world. After going back and witnessing all the pain and devastation my people were suffering, God made it so once again.

My American brothers and sisters rallied around this vision in an overwhelming way.

One time, before a church concert, I watched a father take the shoes right off of his two-year-old daughter and hand them to me. "Go bless someone," he told me. I stared at him, taken off guard. I wrapped those shoes around my neck and wore them for the rest of the night. The tiny ornaments rattled against my heart as I played on the stage, reminding me of how they would protect each steady footstep of a girl in need.

Kids would come up to me after concerts and hand me the shoes they picked out themselves for a Congolese child. It meant the world to me. I felt like I was that little refugee boy again and that these children were reaching me in my time of need, offering a lifesaving gift. In their innocent eyes, I saw the belief that they could change the world. Those kids understood the value of helping someone else.

I reached out to some middle and elementary schools to host "A Day Without Shoes" events. The schools would host shoe drives and bring me and my siblings in for an assembly. We would dance in grass skirts, singing in Mashi over banging drums. We'd share our story, explaining the hardships we faced as kids, walking to school over rocks and parasites, our feet swelling up with infection.

Sometimes, schools would have the kids take their shoes off in the auditorium to relate to the experience. One school, Millis Road Elementary School in Jamestown, North Carolina, set up a tarp in a hallway and covered it with sand. As the kids took off their shoes and walked across it, feeling the coarse grains against their skin, I would ask them, "Would you want to walk like that for the rest of your life?" They would shake their heads or yell, "Nooooo," in childish laughter. I would be able to tell them about how painful it is when your feet are torn up by the ground, harder and bumpier than what they walked on. I could see their eyes open wider in understanding, seeing how blessed they were. I told them to imagine how good it would feel for a kid who has gone their whole life without shoes to slip a pair on for the first time.

Millis Road still sends me shoes every year; I'm so thankful for them.

Over two years, the shoe collection took over the house. It started in my room, which I pretty much gave up. Sometimes I would come home in the middle of the night, exhausted, and have to shove a stack of boxes onto the floor so that I could sleep in my bed. Soon, the boxes multiplied, filling every closet and shrinking the living room. Our house was turned into storage.

Me and my family recognized that this was all for a good cause and saw the mountains of shoeboxes as multiplying blessings. God kept expanding my vision and blowing my mind. Eventually, we had too many shoes for the house and had to move them into a rented space.

At this point, I realized that I had to find a way to get them overseas. I couldn't keep filling up storage units. In the Congo, my network of pastors was waiting, ready to help me distribute. But when I looked up the cost of a shipping container—thirteen thousand dollars—the land and ocean between the U.S. and Congo expanded. Everything was collected on one end, organized on the other, but in-between was a looming obstacle—a mountain only the Lord could move.

My family reminded me of all the miracles God had done for us before. They helped me believe—that amazing things were still to come, that the shoes would make it to the children of the Congo.

We had faith. But we needed help.

Chapter Fifteen

Kick'n It for a Cause
2016-2017

Pastor David's eyes gleamed golden brown in the Virginia sun. The glass walls of Liberty's giant library sparkled behind him as I told him my story on a bench outside the giant silver dome where Convocation is held. It was Thursday, Nov. 17, 2016—which is important to the story—and an unusually warm afternoon. Even though the trees were almost all bare, the grass was still alive and green.

David Nasser was the Senior Vice President for Spiritual Development at Liberty University. To us students, he was our campus pastor—a role he takes very seriously. Even as he hosts one celebrity guest after another, and manages multiple departments, Pastor David always carved out time to spend with students. He even gave out his cell phone number for students to reach him. I knew classmates who received responses late in the night, words of encouragement while they worried over the news that a parent had cancer, or a friend was injured in a car wreck.

He often meets with students one-on-one, but with over thirteen thousand students on campus, it's not something everyone gets to do. Before I contacted him, I remember I was sitting at my desk, concentrating on my homework, when I got this pull, deep in my gut, telling me to reach out to him. For me, it was a step of faith to email him. So, sitting across from him, only about a week later, almost didn't feel real.

It was such a beautiful day. When I met Pastor David at his office, he suggested we go outside, sitting at a table atop the man-made waterfall behind the arena, the Blue Ridge Mountains rippling over the sky in the distance.

I was nervous, but my tongue was lighter than the air outside. I just shared my heart. As Pastor David leaned in, nodding, I told him my story and about the work the Ntibonera Foundation was doing. I sensed the Holy Spirit carrying my words to him. When I explained my predicament about the shipping container, Pastor David creased his forehead and started bouncing questions off of me. Pastor David seemed impressed by how organized I was. He asked about the shipping container. I used my hands to block out a long rectangle to show the dimensions—about the size of the back of a semi-truck. He asked why it was so expensive. I told him it was a flat rate based on size. Pastor David paused, hands pressed together.

He raised a finger to his lips. "How many shoes would fit in that shipping container?"

I told him about twenty thousand.

"And you and your family have raised ten thousand already?"

I nodded.

Pastor David's eyes flashed as he arched his eyebrows. "What if we double your shoe game?"

The words hit me like a bolt of lightning. I couldn't speak. My heart just pounded while time raced by. "What?" slipped out before I composed myself. "Yes sir, I would love that."

One side of his mouth bent upward when he grinned, "Let's do this."

Pastor David marched us back to his office and the whole way I could see ideas racing through his head like cars on a freeway. He isn't a tall man, but when he's focused, he swells with intensity, like a lion. He called everyone who was working in his department together and told them to start planning an event. I still could not believe I had a meeting with him. What was happening around me was beyond unbelievable.

While the long, wooden conference table in his office buzzed with activity, I sunk into my memories. I remembered hiding under my family's table as the world around me erupted in violence. I remembered running in fear, through crowds and chaos. I remembered leaving everything I knew behind. I remembered living a life of desperation: hungry, penniless. I remembered waiting and the heartbreak. I remembered everything changing and coming full circle to realize nothing had changed for my people. I remembered feeling helpless. Determined. Driven. Overwhelmed.

I remembered telling my friends at Liberty that one day I wanted to host a shoe drive in Convocation. I remembered I had no idea when it would happen or how I would pull it off, but I remembered, too, that I had faith.

Sitting in that meeting with Pastor David and his staff, I kept praising God. I knew He had saved me from my former life for a time such as this. What was too difficult for me to accomplish on my own, the Lord orchestrated, right there in front of my eyes.

I saw God.

The very people who had inspired me with the powerful, captivating events they coordinated each week were discussing ways to get an entire university to rally around the Congo. My dream was becoming a reality.

Maybe it was half an hour, maybe a few hours, all I know is that when the big meeting was over, I ran straight to the apartment to find John and tell him what had happened (Baraka was taking a break from school at the time). He could not believe it. We stayed up late that night praising God.

As Christmas break approached, I couldn't wait to go home and share my joy with my family. Our shoe drive was scheduled for the spring semester.

Sitting at home one day during Christmas break, I got a call from Pastor David. He told me that I was on speakerphone. My heart skipped a beat; I had no idea what to expect. He asked me, "Are you ready?" I responded, "Yes sir, I am ready." I was standing, listening attentively.

"Stephen Curry is coming to support your shoe drive."

I collapsed, falling to my knees. The NBA's two-time Most Valuable Player was going to help with my shoe drive? That was unreal to me.

I couldn't even wait for Nasser to stop talking, I cried out, "Thank you, Jesus," right over the phone.

When I was building my foundation, trying to start something to help my people, I saw myself as small, not worthy of making much of an impact. But God saw me differently. I decided to be faithful with my calling, no matter how tiny of a ripple it made, and the Lord used that to flood an arena for His glory. He arranged events to line up perfectly to make a huge impact on his people in the Congo.

Pastor David explained to me that the very next day after our meeting—Friday, Nov. 18, 2016—Ayesha Curry, Stephen's wife, came to speak at Liberty. During the visit, Nasser met Chris "COSeezy"

Strachan, a close friend of the Curry's who also happened to be a Liberty alumnus.

At a luncheon after Ayesha's speech, Pastor David noticed the logo on Chris's hat: "Kick'n It" stitched in the shape of a shoe. He asked Strachan what that was all about. Chris explained that he founded a lifestyle brand that uses his love for sneakers as a tool to bring pop culture and community service together. Kick'n It is more than a company or a charitable organization—it is a movement focused on reaching inner-city kids and teens through pop culture and fashion with the purpose of bettering communities and developing self-confidence to combat bullying and social media negativity.

God was there in the room.

Though worlds apart, our causes had a strong link. Both were focused on people, those society writes off—his in crowded urban cities and mine in villages far removed from society. And both were focused on shoes.

One thing I find incredible about Chris is that he has built this brand to change people's lives. He is very well connected in the worlds of sports, fashion, and the arts. At one of his events, you might find yourself playing video games next to a professional athlete and witness the unveiling of a brand-new sneaker, all while hearing live music from an up-and-coming hip-hop artist. But Chris's events are used to promote small businesses, strengthen communities, feed and clothe the homeless, and collect shoes for underprivileged kids. He doesn't use his connections to build himself up; he does it to build the world up.

Right away, everything Chris was saying fired connections inside Pastor David's brain—he knew that Kick'n It was exactly what my shoe drive at Liberty needed. In his mind, things started to fall into place.

Hearing all of this, I could hardly breathe. I was still on my knees because the news was almost too much to handle. As soon as the conversation ended, I had to catch my breath. I just sat there on the floor, thanking God. Minutes ticked by before I regained my strength and rushed to the living room to tell my family. Of course, there was a celebration, and, like always, we prayed together and praised God.

This is something you don't often hear from students, but I could not wait for school to get back in session.

I connected with Chris on Instagram, and we immediately started to brainstorm the event. Chris is a genius with event planning, promotion, and social media. He envisioned this event going viral, like the Ice Bucket Challenge. We developed a hashtag, #KickNitForACause, and sent videos out all across the major social media networks. We asked people to make their own videos showing the pair of shoes that they would donate and challenging three friends to do the same. So, in reality, the shoe drive launched weeks before March 1, 2017, when Liberty hosted the Convocation.

Boxes started pouring in to the university. Every single day, more and more arrived at Liberty.

As I worked with the Convo planning team to prepare for the event, I learned that Stephen Curry was personally donating five hundred pairs of shoes. I was overwhelmed once again—the only words I could muster were, "Thank you, Jesus." And I learned that his sponsor, Under Armour, was matching the donation, five hundred more. I ran out of words to say.

Gleaning for the World, an international humanitarian organization that meets the needs of those affected by disaster or extreme poverty, worked with me to make the shipping arrangements. My family moved the ten thousand pairs we had collected to the organization's headquarters in Concord, Virginia, not far from Liberty, so that we could store them together with everything we collected with Kick'n It.

Right before the big day, a fifth-grade girl in North Carolina named Hannah volunteered to hold a shoe drive at her school. She collected nine hundred pairs for the people of the Congo! It was incredible what Hannah did, driven by her generous spirit. I hope that God blesses her as much as she has blessed others.

I remember the night before the big day. People were hanging shoes—hundreds, thousands—all around the concourse of the arena, creating a vivid display of color and style. These had been shipped in from all over the country. I could not believe that this was happening. I was humbled to be used by God, honored that I could serve Him.

I remembered kneeling in the African dirt—feeling the earth beneath my legs, the grains of the soil coarse against my flesh—praying that God would provide a pair of shoes for me. And here I was, now the vessel God would use to answer thousands of prayers just like that. What mysterious ways God works in! How is one supposed to feel when God has answered your prayers? Grateful? Joyful? Humbled? Still, awestruck? I was all of those things and more; it was indescribable. That quiet moment in the big, empty arena was one of the best of my life.

The day finally came. I still can't believe that Stephen Curry came down to support the cause. It was the middle of the season, and his team, the Golden State Warriors, was based in Oakland, California—all the way on the other side of the country. He was on his off day during a long road trip—in between games against Washington, the night before, and Chicago, the next night. This was just further evidence to me that what seems impossible before the eyes of men is possible with God.

When I met Chris face-to-face, it was as if we had known each other for a long time. A wide smile stretched across his face, above his bow tie. We were already old friends. We had bonded so much in the months and weeks leading up to this day. We became brothers, united, working together to make a difference. Chris is such a great guy—energetic, full of life and with charisma to spare. When he spoke from the stage, he played to the crowd with ease, drawing smiles and causing laughter, shining brightly right alongside one of the NBA's biggest stars. This comfort stems from how genuine Chris is, even in front of such a large audience—there were well over ten thousand people there that day; Liberty had to add risers to the concourse to seat all the guests, and there were people who still had to stand. Chris lives to bring joy to others; he wants to put smiles on people's faces, like the one he always wears. He has such a big heart.

Meeting Stephen was surreal. Here I was, standing before this man I watched playing basketball on TV. And he was here for me, for the people of the Congo. He told me that he was here to support the work we were doing. I was overwhelmed with emotion, humbled, full of gratitude. I was honored to be in the same room as Steph; it blew my mind that God had brought him here to support the vision that had been laid on my heart.

Outside, people lined up and then poured in by the thousands. They dropped shoes into wide, red bins across the concourse.

Backstage, Liberty's representative from Nike had five hundred brand new pairs of shoes for us stacked high in fresh, orange boxes. It was like each pair was designed for a specific person in the Congo.

I have always enjoyed Convocation, but that day was like nothing before. I was just so overwhelmed to watch my entire university community rally around my dream. Everyone was so generous and enthusiastic. I honestly felt that this was the beginning of a movement that could bring change to the Congo.

My entire family was there with me. All my life, they had been a significant source of encouragement and support, and it meant a lot for me to have them there by my side on this momentous day. It was also meaningful to see Stephen—well known for bringing his daughter to press conferences after games—make it a family event as well. Ayesha was there along with his mom, Sonya Curry.

On the stage, Pastor David led a talk-show-style discussion with Stephen, Chris, Sonya, and Ritchie McKay, Liberty's Men's Basketball

Head Coach. McKay became friends with the Curry family years earlier when he recruited Stephen's brother, Seth, to play at Liberty.

There was something relatable about Stephen's words from up on the stage. Our platforms and skills may have been different—he was a superstar professional basketball player, and I was just a former refugee still in college—but at our core, we both exist to serve and honor God.

Stephen told students to be "confident in your abilities and the platform that God has given you in life" and to use that platform "to shine light back to Him."

I know many students, like me, were encouraged by those words.

"That is the only reason I feel like I do what I do, and I've been blessed with the talents to do what I do," Steph continued. "That, hopefully, is first and foremost when you watch me play—you see that light shine through, you see the joy that I have for what I do and the perspective that the Lord has blessed me with these talents to do something special. But it is not about me. That is something that I want my career and my life to be a reflection of … His love and His grace and mercy. Whether I am winning games or losing games, making shots or missing shots, it is all about giving glory to God."

Wow. His commitment to being faithful in basketball reminded me of the one I made to God with my music back when I was a refugee in Kenya. It meant a lot to hear those words coming from someone with so much talent and influence, someone who literally has the eyes of the world on him every day. It encouraged me in my mission as well.

If you watch Stephen play, you'll notice Scripture written on his shoes and see him pointing to Heaven to honor God when he makes shots. Still, it was special seeing his life shine up close. You could see how genuine he was just by looking at his face and listening to his voice. The words he spoke were not empty lip service.

When I listened to Sonya speak, it became apparent that Stephen's faith, while clearly his own, was something he learned at home.

"We're not guaranteed to be here every day, but the Word of God will last forever," she said. "When people disappoint you, and situations disappoint you, you've always got God and the Word."

I was reminded of the lessons my own parents taught me—how no matter what hardships we faced, Mom and Dad always showed us how to trust in the Lord and to pray without ceasing.

"The key to it," Sonya said of raising her children, "is prayer … It works, prayer works."

I could almost hear my own mother's voice—softly, in a dim, candle-lit room.

Another aspect of the Currys' story that resonated with me—which, looking back, I think was evidence of God's divine handiwork—was how people constantly doubted Stephen's ability to succeed as he progressed in his career. His younger brother, Seth (who played at Liberty under McKay for one season), faced similar barriers. As a refugee, I often felt overlooked.

Stephen was not highly sought after by top-tier college basketball programs. Even after bringing Davidson, a smaller college, to the Elite Eight of the NCAA Tournament in 2008 (his team only lost by two points to number one-ranked Kansas), he was still underestimated as a prospect in the 2009 NBA Draft. He was the seventh pick. Today, he is considered one of the greatest shooters of all time, with multiple three-pointer records to his name. In ten years, he was a two-time Most Valuable Player who went to the NBA Finals in five-straight seasons, winning the championship three times.

Like his older brother, Seth did not get a lot of attention out of high school either. He came to play at Liberty and ended up becoming the leading freshman scorer in the country, even as he faced double and even triple defensive coverage night-after-night. Seth finished his career at Duke, one of the nation's premier college basketball programs. Today, he is also playing in the NBA.

"Both of my boys were not highly recruited," Sonya said, looking to Liberty's coach, "and Ritchie, you saw Seth, you saw what was in Seth."

The Curry brothers' example of perseverance helped remind me that it doesn't matter what people think of you; if God gifts you for a purpose, nothing can stop it. You still have to work hard. It won't always be easy, as I can attest from my life on the brink of starvation, but the only opinion about you that matters is what God thinks of you.

It was crazy for me to think, sitting in Liberty's arena that day, how God had used everything that I went through to bring me to a position where I could help countless people facing similar struggles as I once did.

After the encouraging discussion, I was brought down onto the basketball court to join Stephen and the others. Students flooded the edges of the hardwood, reaching over one another at the barricades to snap pictures as Stephen walked by. I could not hear anything over the crowd, but I understood that Pastor David announced that Liberty agreed to help cover the shipping cost for the container and to help my family out with airfare to travel to the Congo that summer. Praise God! But then, Pastor David said Liberty was willing to contribute more money to our cause if the guests, including Stephen and I, made baskets on the court. I was a bit nervous for my turn, knowing that I am not a basketball player.

My heartbeat pounded up my throat and in my ears as the crowd roared and, one by one, people went up to take their shots.

Coach McKay took a free throw. *Miss.* Chris stepped to the line. He also missed. Finally, Liberty's President, Jerry Falwell Jr., sunk a basket, the crowd erupting in response. Ayesha then took a turn, unable to connect.

When Stephen stepped up, he tried a couple of three-pointers but couldn't find his rhythm. Now I was even more nervous—there was no way I could expect to do much better.

My pulse raced as I watched Sonya try, and miss, and Ayesha take another turn, unsuccessfully.

Then, Pastor David called out, "Emmanuel."

My classmates surrounded me, pressed up against the barricades.

"Hey, everything you see today is his fault," Pastor David announced playfully, bouncing me the ball. "Come on, give it up for Emmanuel everybody."

The crowd's roar never ceased, but inside me, I felt a quiet peace, despite my thundering heartbeat. I took the ball, palms sweaty. I squared up at the three-point line, bounced the ball once, then twice, telling God I wanted to make the shot for the children of the Congo. When I flung the ball at the hoop, it rattled a little, but it went in. The crowd went wild. I doubled over with relief and excitement. My heart lightened up in my chest. Chris and Steph each came over to give me a hug. Making that three-pointer was such an incredible feeling, but I knew it was all for the children of the Congo.

Stephen ended the action at half court, missing a long shot but chasing after it to give the crowd a slam dunk to finish what had already been a wild and exciting event.

Liberty was so generous, providing shipping and transportation funds, and, when all was said and done, money for truck rentals in the DRC. I was also blown away by how my classmates, and the whole university community across the country, came together for this cause.

We more than doubled our shoe collection that day—over twenty thousand pairs total.

Chapter Sixteen

Empty Hands
Summer 2017

The beige walls of my hotel room were closing in. I spent hours each day pacing back and forth, dropping to my knees to pray, and then getting up to walk some more circles. My knees were sore from the slick, hard floor. Out the window, palm and banana leaves waved up at me while Bukavu remained still. People and cars may have filled the streets, but to me, nothing was moving; even Lake Kivu seemed to have stilled its waves. Nothing was coming into the Congo. Life had frozen. That's how it felt to me, at least.

I had been in my motherland for two weeks and, still, had nothing to show for all my hard work the past two years. My truckload of shoes had disappeared. It was somewhere between the Eastern shore of the United States and Tanzania, on the east side of Africa. That knowledge didn't help lift my spirits, which had sunk to the bottom of the Atlantic.

Stuck in that room, which felt like a prison cell, with nothing to bring the people I had vowed to help, it felt like ages had gone by since Stephen Curry patted me on the shoulder to tell me he appreciated the work I was doing. That was March. In June, I remember waking up early on a Wednesday, sunbeams poking through the wall of trees beside me as I drove over to Gleaning for the World's headquarters. The warehouse was a massive metal cavern, filled with pallets of supplies, ready to ship out to anywhere in the world at a moment's notice, offering relief to storm victims.

I spent many days in that warehouse.

Steph left not long after Convocation was over on March 1. That evening, Pastor David invited my family's band to perform during a campus worship service. Chris and I then sunk into a leather couch across from him on the stage, Pastor David's eyes burning with intensity as he asked us questions about our influences and passions. When it was over, Pastor David took up an offering. Students filled buckets with wadded bills from their pockets. These were my classmates, and some were studying at other local colleges. Already they had done so much by helping double my shoe collection in one day. Now, they were sacrificing even more, helping pay for the travel costs of my family's trip to the Congo. Dad closed the night by praying in French. I almost cried in front of everyone.

The day had been long and overwhelming; I was ready to crash. But first I went backstage. Between the high concrete walls, stacks of boxes holding shoes climbed toward the ceiling. Around me, dozens of Liberty students moved past me, carrying more boxes. On the ground, I saw two girls—one with light hair the other dark, pulled up in tails behind their heads—sorting shoes by size, inspecting to make sure the used ones were good enough to wear, before packing them up. The student volunteers stayed up late into the night, helping me load up the boxes to send to the warehouse.

For the next few weeks, I would go to the GFTW warehouse almost every day. I never wanted to miss a moment. I had plenty of help; Liberty volunteers kept coming out to help us fill up our container, now paid for in full by the university. The organization provided volunteers as well, sorting and packing up the donations. Still, John and I wanted to see the project through to the end.

The work set my mind at ease; I could be having the worst day, feeling low, but then walk into that storage facility and put my hands on a pair of sneakers and immediately feel better. My hands would run down the smooth fabrics, feeling the bumps of plastic in the logos and patterns that decorated them. I would think about the life destined to change from that pair and shoot up a quick prayer for the boy or girl destined to wear them. I imagined the children slipping them on over calloused, dirty feet, watching the smiles grow across their faces. Then, I'd pack them away, my soul at peace.

On a Wednesday morning in June, the sky was as wide and clear as a lake, just small ripples of clouds. I stood behind my container, loaded up and rigged to a giant truck, and watched from the dock as it rolled off and disappeared. The journey to the Congo began; It was unbelievable.

On June 28, Dad and Christian arrived in Bukavu. They went ahead of the rest of us so they could meet the container when it arrived the next day. It was going to be all unloaded so that we could begin delivering shoes when I arrived two weeks later.

A day passed, then another, but I didn't hear anything about the shipment. The next time I spoke with Dad on the phone, he told me he still hadn't seen or heard anything about the container, and I started to get rattled.

I thought that I had done all the hard work; this was supposed to be the easy part of the process. Two more weeks went by and I boarded my plane to Africa, still with no word about the shipment.

All I knew is that once the goods were to arrive in Tanzania, they would be loaded up and trucked across the country to Rwanda, and then over to my motherland. Whose hands it had passed through along the way, where it could have ended up, were a mystery.

When I arrived at the Congolese/Rwandan border, my Uncle Bugondo, Dad's brother, walked up and gave me a tight hug. He started to reach for my brothers, John and Baraka, and then froze when he saw Mom and Adili standing right behind us. He had almost overlooked them because he was not expecting to see them. We had kept their coming a secret. Uncle Bugondo blinked his eyes hard a few times to make sure he was seeing clearly. Then he wrapped them up in a big hug.

About a hundred family members and friends were waiting to greet us at my Aunt Regina's house. They were as shocked as Uncle Bugondo to see Mom and Adili there with us. Everyone got so emotional, people crying everywhere, pushing up behind each other to get their hugs. Mom's big smile kept pushing down sobs. I have never seen her so happy. We celebrated late into the night before heading to our hotel, where I collapsed inside the gray, stone tower.

I was supposed to be off to work but my container was more than two weeks late. I had a church choir and about seventy volunteers all ready to go. We had a train of trucks prepared to pack up and dig into the jungle for the big delivery. But all I could do was wait.

I waited for two weeks. Nothing but empty hands. It's strange how heavy that felt; I could hardly raise my arms, or even shrug my shoulders.

If I wasn't locking myself away from everybody else, stewing or praying, I was sending messages trying to track down the shipment. It was more than four weeks since the load was supposed to have arrived and I couldn't get any answers from the shipping company. I felt betrayed, lied to. I was frustrated and upset. Over unreliable internet I reached out for help, asking my sisters and friends back home for prayer and emotional support.

My fear and worry weighed down on me more each day. Time was running out. *What if the container never makes it?* I wondered. I was so frustrated that it unraveled my mind. I could only imagine who had gotten their hands on the shoes and what they were going to do with them. *Maybe they were stolen. What would I do then?* I was breaking down. Time was running out.

My trip was planned to be nineteen days long. Each one passed by. I felt disconnected from the outside world—because I had withdrawn and because it was hard to get online.

Alone, with the curtains drawn, I begged God to have mercy on me for my doubt. I knew the tearing pain inside me, filling me with darkness, was the Devil clawing at me, looking for a foothold. The enemy wanted to scare me and discourage me from my work.

My visa was approved for a month. I determined to use up whatever time I had to figure out a way to find my container and get the shoes delivered to children in the villages.

I was so stressed that I could hardly eat. I was shedding weight like the sweat that constantly poured from my forehead. My face felt heavy. When I looked in the mirror, I saw a stranger. I questioned who I was, I questioned my calling. I felt like a failure. I had no idea what I would do next, or even what I would tell all the people who had rallied behind me. Alone, in my darkness, I feared that people would think that I had raised all of those shoes as a scheme. My reputation would be ruined along with all of the good work I was trying to do.

While I was suffering, I knew that my dad and brothers carried their own weights as well. I always felt that I needed to be the strong one in our family, to help lift what pressed down on everyone else so that they could breathe easier. But I was completely worn out. The sick one of the herd, I was ready to lie down and let the hunting beast consume me.

Mom sensed my struggle and came to my side. She warmed me with her delicate smile as she put an arm around my shoulders and started praying. Mom's words were sweet like honey, soothing my soul, and they erupted like fire as she rebuked Satan. Empowered, I unleashed the force of my pain and struggle in a cry to God, echoing Mom's blows against the evil one. Then, I collapsed and told God that I needed Him now more than ever.

My visa was looking over the edge of a cliff. All of my plans had been rearranged, events moved, rescheduled, and then cancelled until further notice. My shipment was lost.

I received word during that final week that Pastor David, Chris, and some other friends of mine from Liberty were in Africa. Liberty was laying the groundwork for its first yearlong impact initiative—G5, which started in Rwanda. The leaders wanted to meet me at the border.

It was a risk—I could lose my visa—but I needed the encouragement. I was in such a dark place.

Kivu's waves slapped each other while guards eyed me with distrusting eyes when I approached the international bridge. When I was questioned at the gate, one of the officers accused me and my brother of being spies. I held up my empty hands. I had nothing to offer but the passport on the table in front of them.

Through a tangle of metal across the way, I could see Chris' wide smile almost covering the rest of the team. We could only stand there and wave at each other through the fence at first.

Finally, the guards let me pass. They told me I had fifteen minutes and that I couldn't take a single picture. I didn't care, I was so relieved.

Stepping over the wide concrete suspended above the waters was like gliding over a razor's edge. But then I reached the four men coming the other way and felt a little better, even though my shoulders were still drawn tight, aware of the eyes on me.

Chris told me how he had taken a few thousand pairs of shoes to Congolese refugees in Rwandan camps. He had so much energy; he was thrilled to be in the land of his ancestors. "We did it!" He told me.

I told the group that I didn't have the container on my side yet and confessed that my faith was holding together by a thread.

Pastor David's eyes met mine with a knowing glance. He's a U.S. immigrant, too. His family had to flee political violence in Iran. I could relate to him on so many levels; just being with him washed away so much of my unease. He patted my shoulders, relieving some of the burden as he and Joshua Rutledge, Liberty's Vice President of Spiritual Development, prayed over me. Steven Gillum, Director of LU Serve International, the guy who leads Liberty's international engagement efforts, told me that I had an army of people behind me, praying and believing in the mission. Joshua assured me that everything would work out.

It felt comforting to know these people would stick by me.

I floated back to the Congolese side of the bridge, feeling lighter than before. A day before we were supposed to leave, I told my family that I had decided to stay for seven more days. We all cancelled our flights.

Still, my thread of faith was being pulled to its breaking point. I remember one night waking up and just crying out to God. There were no words, just hollow breaths. I was at my end.

Two days later, I finally got word about my container. It was in the Congo, at the port of entry! I was baptized by relief. My bonds snapped, setting me free of the tension, and I rushed out the door.

I learned that all along the container was not in transit, as I was being told, but held up by the men responsible for it. My container sat at the border of Tanzania and Rwanda collecting dust, all over ten dollars. It was a fee for some paperwork. I was frustrated because I had a friend on standby ready to pay any money needed to get the container through. The men working wouldn't even let him pay the small fee; they just took their time. In the United States, there are expectations for how a business is to be run. Not so in Africa: people in some countries work at their own pace, no rush at all. Unbelievable.

When I got to the port, I was on guard, like a boxer, ready for a struggle. I expected to encounter corruption. The reality in the Congo is that you could walk into the office on any given day and be told a different price, at the whim of whoever was working at that moment. You would not even get a receipt. You just have to come prepared to bargain.

But that day, God was on my side. Donors to the Ntibonera Foundation had lined my pocket with enough money to clear the customs fees, and the shipment was released quickly and smoothly.

We left under the darkness of night and drove the truckload of supplies from the shipyard to the gated office compound where the Ntibonera Foundation had arranged storage.

Tired as we were, the first thing we did when we got back was bow our heads in prayer. Then, it was off for a couple hours of sleep. At four a.m. the next morning we unlocked the door to the container, raised the metal arm holding everything inside, and started unloading the boxes. It took sixty people and two hours to complete the job. We moved fast, aware of the ticking clock.

We were going to cram fifteen days of work into five.

Chapter Seventeen
Father to the Fatherless
Summer 2017

The lump in my throat rose and fell with the bumps in the road as my body rattled around inside the cab of a large rented truck. I'd been up since three a.m., but my eyes fixed on the path ahead. I was excited.

John was by my side, between me and the driver. Behind us in the truck bed, sitting on a tarp stretched over a mountain of shoes, Baraka and Christian held onto the sides of the truck along with several volunteers.

We left under the darkness of night. The trip to Kaziba—where I had lived for a year with my family, hiding from the war—would have been about forty-five minutes on a paved highway. Since the road was bare and unkept, however, it took four hours. The ride from the city into the jungle was an adventure, the ground rolling us like choppy waters tossing a boat to sea.

Grandpa Ntibonera was ninety-years-old when we arrived at his house to pick him up. Even though he had to be taken out in a wheelchair, I saw strength in him. He kept his head high as we pushed him outside. He is the real Ntibonera, the original; all of the foundation's work is due to his legacy. He taught my dad generosity with the way he loved his people and served his community, always donating from the abundance of his harvests. I witnessed that kindness myself. It was important for me to show him the work that was going on in his name—his name and, more importantly, the name of the God he taught us to serve.

Grandpa's face lit up faster than the sky above the tree line as he watched nearly seventy villagers gather around him. I placed a pair of sneakers in his grip—small ones, not much bigger than his hands. I gave him the honor of handing out the first set of shoes from the drive. He placed the first pair in a young boy's hands. The boy smiled from ear-to-ear as he slid his feet into the gift and ran over the infested ground, protected. Grandpa kept handing out shoes, one pair at a time, his grip firm as he placed them in each set of hands. "Go, and serve others like that," he would commission each gift. I saw the love that Grandpa had for his neighbors pouring out like the rains that nourished his crops. It was the perfect moment to kick off the distribution. Forty-five children and twenty adults walked away with bold strides, disappearing into the dark green forest as they ran and leapt back home.

The sun baked an open field where my team of volunteers finished setting up for the day's main event. One thousand children had gathered outside a Catholic school. Kids started chasing after our convoy as we rolled in. They smiled and shouted as the tires chewed through the road right past them; they had never seen such a sight before.

I didn't see a single pair of shoes as my eyes scanned the crowd. The rot and decay of infection marked several feet. The sight brought an ache to my chest as I tried to listen while Dad opened the event with a prayer and quick message about God's love for each person there. When I raised my eyes higher, the endless stream of smiles soothed my heart. The children could hardly stand still as they listened to Dad tell them that we had a gift for them: a token to help them realize the unending gift God offers each one of us, a pair of shoes that will protect their feet like the way Jesus guards the souls of his children.

We lined everyone up through a snaked rope path and handed each student and teacher a ticket. The tickets helped us make sure that the people we were there to serve were indeed served, ahead of anyone else who might turn up as the distribution went on.

It was wild—wildly amazing—as bodies poured from the ropes to our boxes. Bending down, lacing up fresh sneakers over a small, crusty pair of feet, swelled my heart. My field of vision was blurred with bright blues and streaks of pink, yellow, and green. Here were children who—most, if not all—had never owned a pair of shoes before, running around in Nikes, Under Armours, and Jordans that would be the envy of American children. But for the Congolese children, a pair of shoes was a treasure, not a fleeting status symbol to be discarded for the next trend. It wasn't about a brand, logo, or label there; it was about protection, vitality. About hope.

We sent the children off with a blessing from God and a charge to not miss school now that their feet were protected from infections.

The kids started running home, spraying dirt into the air as they called out to their friends and neighbors in the village. The crowd multiplied. We had handed out two thousand tickets before we started, and once they were all collected, I kept tying up shoes around feet as they wandered in. I had planned for this. Our trucks carried enough sets for thirty-five hundred people. But as shoe after shoe punched the ground and disappeared behind me, the crowd before me only grew. Soon, there was nothing left to give. It wasn't easy knowing some people left empty-handed, but I felt blown away by a whirlwind; all the stomping and running in circles around me told me how well the distribution went.

News was spreading like wildfire as we climbed into our vehicles. I could hear people asking, "Who are these people giving out free shoes?" The villagers had never seen such a thing. When we drove off, kids chased after us screaming "Thank you," rubber wings flying them over the ground.

Time was short, so we drove straight to an orphanage to bring clothes, shoes, and food for the children there.

I crumbled inside, worse than the state of condition the room was in, when I walked in. Cries filled the room. There were more babies than arms to hold them. Tears welled up in my eyes. The children—fifty-one total, from babies to seven-years-old—were weak and showing signs of malnutrition. Several of them coughed or had trails running from their noses as they sat bunched together on the floor, all barefoot. The first thing I did was make sure that each child had a new pair of shoes put on their feet. Then, I watched their eyes grow, their mouths erupt with teeth as I brought out toys for them, donated by Gleaning for the World. The kids found their energy and started bouncing around me. I broke down and started crying as we handed out the gifts. I started hugging each of them until I was surrounded by skinny arms and little faces. I wanted each one to know that I loved them.

I met with the women who ran the facility. They told me that the orphanage was supposed to be under the supervision of the hospital, but there was hardly any support. The hospital served a population of over one hundred thousand and was in terrible condition on its own.

The only reason the orphanage had been started in the first place was because so many women died during childbirth. Some women, fearing they could not care for their child, would give birth and then walk over to the orphanage and drop the child outside before slipping away. They believed leaving them would give the kids a better chance at being cared for. Other children were orphaned by the war or AIDS. And there were those who were the result of rape, abandoned out of pain or fear of shame.

The women took care of the growing number of children as best they could, even though money was not coming in. They were supposed to be paid twenty dollars per month. Sometimes they made less, other months they didn't get paid at all. But the dedicated women continued their work whether or not they got paid because they love the children so much. I couldn't believe how little they were expected to live on, especially after I learned many of them had children of their own.

While the workers struggled to put food in each of the young mouths, the director did his best to collect donations. What little comes in is not enough. He did tell me, however, that thirty-two orphans had been adopted by Americans. I was pleased to hear that the love and kindness of my new countrymen had reached this far.

The workers saw my foundation as a miracle; in addition to the shoes and clothes, we provided them with food, cooking oil, and soap. Around the workers' smiles, I saw the fatigue worn deep in their faces. My team and I stayed for a couple hours, giving the women a break.

As the caretakers relaxed, my brothers helped the kids play with their new toys. I picked up the babies and held them in my arms. I looked into their innocent faces, thin and fragile. While rocking one girl, so small and only three months old, I recalled the words of the psalmist: *A father to the fatherless, a defender of widows, is God in His holy dwelling* (Psalm 68:5, NIV). It was a precious moment.

I looked up and watched the other children, running around, breaking in their new shoes and wrestling with my brothers.

I went over to the hospital and visited the maternity ward. Inside, the walls cracked with peeling paint. There were hardly any beds in the entire hospital; I walked around and saw the sick wrapped in blankets, sleeping on the floor. Women often had to deliver their babies on the floor, just a mat beneath them.

There was hardly any electricity in the entire facility—only a small generator kept for night emergencies. The hospital tried not to keep patients there at night because it was so dark. One doctor told me they often would treat their patients by candlelight.

To disinfect equipment, the staff just used boiling water. They didn't even have enough scissors to go around for operations; the doctors just scraped together whatever instruments they could find.

I felt like a cancer was eating away inside me as I witnessed the state of things, wondering how anyone could be treated effectively in there. Like the orphanage, the hospital couldn't afford to pay all of the doctors and the nurses.

Before it got too late, I ran back to the orphanage one more time to hug the children again. I almost drowned beneath them.

When I stood up, the director met me, eye to eye. The hollowness behind his gaze had been filled. As his eyes sparkled, the director asked me if the Ntibonera Foundation could become the fathers and mothers to the fifty-one children in the room. He'd never witnessed generosity like ours before and told me that he believed we had been sent there to save the orphanage.

It had taken me two years to collect enough supplies for one giant distribution campaign. Most of that time, I didn't even know how I was going to get the stuff to the Congo. The responsibility of taking over an orphanage was too much for me to bring back home with me. But I knew that the weight was not going to fall on my shoulders alone—I remembered how God had overpowered any obstacle I thought would derail my vision. So, as I set back down the bumpy road for the four-hour return journey to Bukavu, I carried the orphanage's burden with me. I'd agreed to support it.

Chapter Eighteen

Shoeprints
Summer 2017

Tires spit a cloud of dust against the faintly glowing horizon behind us. The sky was a silver sheet when we crashed through the thick, damp brush leading to Chibuga, the Pygmy village at five a.m. the next morning.

The governor of South Kivu, the province where all of my work took place and the land of my childhood, and a congressman joined me on the journey, along with a security escort. Bags swelled under my eyes; I'd barely had enough time to clean up and rest from the trip to Kaziba.

But I was keeping my promise.

Two trucks barreled over the dirt, weighed down by more than ten thousand pairs of shoes. Two more were loaded up with rice, beans, and salt while a minibus chased them down a road that turned from a rusty tan to deep chocolate as the jungle grew up around us. I had a choir and seventy volunteers with me. This was going to be big.

The Chibugan villagers had cleared a path for our caravan. Word had reached them that I was returning. The road still flung me up and down, but I was proud of how the people had tried to make it easier for me to arrive than when I had in 2015.

Kids sprinted alongside our monstrous metal box vehicles, eyes wide with wonder. I've never seen such joy. People ran out of their huts, forming a welcome train behind the vehicles, dancing, clapping, and singing.

I was surrounded by a chorus of Pygmy voices, their feet pounding the soil in a percussive rhythm.

"Ahadi Ya Mungu haibadiliki! Ahadi Ya Mungu haibadiliki! Ahadi Ya Mungu haibadiliki!

The words floated all around us, swirling in harmony with the breeze. My choir sang along out the windows. John jumped down from the truck and joined the growing crowd of people, singing the same words, over and over as they paraded down the road. The Pygmies kept chanting, repeating the same Swahili phrase, which means "The promises of God never change."

Over the symphony, our team set up a tent and prepared to begin the largest shoe distribution in Congo's history. Before we began, a giant church service broke out, right there in the field. I felt God's presence heavy upon us all, thicker than the clouds holding back the sky overhead.

Dad started speaking, and I was caught up by the beauty of the moment—dense green foliage surrounding us, a canvas of the Maker's handiwork, as thousands of his children congregated to worship Him.

When I got up to speak, I told everyone that our sole purpose, the reason that we exist in the world, is to worship God.

After the service, I was given a tour of the village. My family was invited deeper than anyone had been before to see for ourselves how these people lived. The Chibugan villagers marched after us, voices still chanting praises in harmony, as my eyes were ripped wide open. I couldn't believe what I was seeing; I thought that I had witnessed suffering the last time I was in the village, but that was only the beginning.

All over the place, kids were lying, hardly able to move due to starvation. Their skin looked like it was trying to eat up their bones. Some were paralyzed, legs shriveled like uprooted tubers as they sat helpless on the ground. They had never, in their entire lives, seen a doctor.

I met children so ravaged by infection that they had no strength; they had been left behind while everyone else went to the field for the distribution. No one carried them along. Me and my volunteers began picking them up, one-by-one. This was the image of God, and I could not bear to see it, to see them, dying of hunger. We started feeding them and putting shoes on their feet, serving them before anyone else.

Behind me, I heard a new verse rise out of the stream of music flowing behind me: "*Mungu amejibu Maombi yetu*," God has finally answered our prayers. The melody haunted me.

I do not think that I saw a single child whose feet were not bare and infected. The village leaders told me that children die there every single day. I thought about how pets in America are better taken care of than these people—meals, shelter, medical treatment.

My heart broke as I spoke with the children. Some had not eaten in four days. They were filthy; they never bathe, and their clothes were worn down to barely even rags. Though some days I had forgotten what it was like—spoiled by my daily showers, three meals a day, possessions in excess—I had lived this life before. I could relate to their stories. I had been there.

I saw hopelessness. No food, hardly any shelter. If it rained, the villagers suffered; when it was hot, they suffered. No water nearby; they had to walk for miles to get it. I could not believe the conditions that the government expected these people—once stable hunters and gatherers—to live in. No land to raise crops. Since they were unable to farm, they resorted to stealing from farms in neighboring villages, causing fights to break out between them and their neighbors.

People young and old had packed the clearing, as if the jungle had overgrown it, in the minutes I had been gone. As we prepared to start the distribution, Dad stood up and preached a message of hope. I was there to bring people shoes, but my foundation had a bigger mission, too. Christ's love was the best gift we could give them. I knew that God was the only one who could bring true, boundless fulfillment to the lives I touched. At least seventy people surrendered their lives to Christ that day—many of them did not believe in any sort of god at all before that moment.

Once the distribution started, the people could hardly be contained. Fights broke out as they rushed to get their hands on something, anything. It was crazy. I am beyond thankful to the volunteers who helped keep the order that day and made the event possible.

The goods were divided into three sections: one for food, one for clothes, and the other for shoes. We had to use tickets again to prevent people from taking what was meant for others. We served those with tickets first and then gave out whatever we had left to everyone else.

First, I was helping fit people into a new pair of shoes, but then I moved over to where food was being given out. It was a punch in the gut. Tears streamed down faces as people came up to get supplies. I watched women struggle to carry their malnourished children as they were crying in pain from infected toes. I remember one mother setting a child down, off her back, so that she could pick up her food. The little girl tore the sky with her screams, reaching up for her mom. She was not even a year old, and already her toes were all gone. I took a deep breath as that image burned into my mind and sent hot tears down my face. I ran over and pulled the family aside, out of the way so I could give them some extra food. When they disappeared, I had to focus on my breathing to compose myself. There were so many painful images flashing before my eyes—I could hardly stand it all.

The volunteers were working tirelessly with no chance to take a break. I opened up my bag and watched the children flock to me as I started handing out candies. There were so many little hands grabbing at me that my brothers had to help me make sure that everyone got one.

After the sweets were gone, one of my volunteers carried a three-year-old girl over to me, crying with pain. I could tell right away that she did not have much time left to live. Infections had overrun her body. I went close and held her hands, tender with rotting flesh. Her knees had been eaten away. She had no toenails. Her stomach had inflated like a balloon, bloated from kwashiorkor, severe nutritional deficiency. With the girl in my hands suffering, I wept and prayed for Jesus to save her. Her body hardly put any strain on my arms as I wrapped her in them. I made sure to give her mother as much supplies as we could.

When I made my way back through the lines, I found an elderly couple who kept getting pushed aside by younger people pressing past them to move ahead. I took their trembling arms and led the couple to the front of the line and made sure they were provided for.

We served the entire village. The tickets were very important in helping me make sure that I did this, so that the people of Chibuga knew I had kept my promise. I had to start with the people who I had come to serve. Villagers from all across the area started to file in through the trees. It was not that I didn't want to help them all, but the supplies were limited. As more and more people crammed into the clearing, we kept serving them until there was nothing left.

People started fighting over the empty shoeboxes. The volunteers threw the boxes into the air just to get away. Hands grabbed at them in a frenzy, like wild dogs on a carcass. When the chaos subsided, I asked someone why people were so desperate for the boxes. They told me it was so that they could cut them open, lay them flat, and use them to sleep on. Words failed me in searching for a response.

Looking around me, my eyes opened more and more to the needs of my people. Villagers were still pouring in, even as we had nothing left to give. I promised to send a team with more shoes and clothes.

John also donated some musical instruments to the village church; he told them to carry on the song of praise that they had welcomed us with.

It was nighttime before we made it back to our hotel.

Because time was limited, my plans to host several mini-distributions through local churches in Bukavu were scrapped. Instead, we hosted all of the churches, both ones that partnered with my organization and ones I hadn't worked with before, in one place.

We packed out the wide, modern sanctuary of M.C.A.P. Eglises with six church bodies from different denominations. The sea of voices added a deep, swelling layer to the music that rolled up onto the stage where my family played with the choir. The instrumentation blared from the speakers in a sweet eruption, rising up to one God.

The giant church service lasted for three hours. Me and my family told the congregations that we were bringing everyone together as a show of unity, hoping they could go out and do the same thing in the Congo. There was so much bitterness and distrust after the years of fighting and so many people blaming others for the problems in the country. I encouraged the congregants to move on, to forgive and to love one another. I wanted to see the church come together to help build up the country.

Later in the day, a crowd assembled around a grungy, concrete court while I met with a traveling basketball team. The players told me that they just want people to have fun and to show kids that there is hope. So many boys still believed that the only way to make a living is to join up with rebels.

I gave the players shoes, including a size seventeen to a tree of a man. He was the only person in all of Bukavu who fit into them. The team put on an exhibition game and I listened, over the roar of the crowd, as the sneakers squeaked across the ground.

Our last day of distribution was a Tuesday. My cousins took me to the streets that ran behind a row of hotels to find a pack of former child soldiers who had been rescued by the U.N. I watched as they fished through garbage cans and slinked over to street corners to beg for food before being chased off by hotel workers.

My brothers and I called them over, about twenty-five in all, offering them juice and bread. They wiped their hands on the sides of their pants, which probably had more dirt than their palms, and dug in. I learned that these boys struggled to fit in; many of them couldn't go back to their families because their minds had been so warped by the horrors they endured. Their own families feared them. They were left to just wander the streets.

The boys stuck together—at night they slept at a shelter and during the day they ran wild. All they had were each other.

Some of the boys had been grabbed right off the streets. In my mind, I saw John, not yet ten-years-old, nearing a muddy truck across the field where we were playing soccer more than a decade earlier. My hand jerked instinctively; I almost grabbed John's grown-up hand beside me, and I realized that their story could have been his story. It could have been my story, too.

Rebels abduct kids as young as eight, sometimes even younger, forcing them to take an oath to fight for their cause. The boys are then drugged. This is how they are welcomed to their new "family." My eyes grew wide and I had to choke down the bile welling up inside my gut as the kids explained the terrible things they were forced to do. The rebels make them start killing—imagine, a seven-year-old forced to hold a gun and start taking lives—and also raping women. Insanity. These stories tore my heart. I read the pain written in their eyes as they spoke. Their high, childish voices sunk with a weight beyond their years.

I wanted to cry—they were just children! Now, all they wanted to do was go back home. But their families did not want them.

Roaming the streets, they can barely care for themselves. They can't afford school. They beg and dig through garbage to stay fed.

After devouring all of the food we brought, crumbs rolling down their chins, I turned on the radio. My brothers started dancing. The boys joined in as the African beats rolled through our bodies, our feet kicking out in response. There were no choreographed steps, just freestyle dancing, letting the beat control our bodies like puppets. Freestyle is a great way to lose yourself and forget your troubles.

I watched the uncaged joy leap and twist around in the open street, in the growing shadows of the hotels. I didn't want that afternoon to end. Those boys, they just wanted to live like other boys and girls. They needed love. I made sure to fit each one in a pair of shoes before I had to go. They begged us to take them with us. I sighed; *I wish*. I flipped the radio back on and danced one last song with them, willing the sun to stand still. I prayed that there would be a way I could provide for these and other forgotten people long-term.

News of my foundation's work flooded the entire city of Bukavu. Nothing like that had ever been done in the country's history. Like bees to a field of flowers, people buzzed outside my hotel. Some were trying to score a pair of shoes, others would tug at my shirt, look up at me, smile with glowing eyes, and express gratitude. I felt a cloud lifting away from above the city.

The last days of my trip evaporated before I could soak in the joy of knowing I had done what I had come back to do. Before our departure,

I held a party to thank the volunteers and security who traveled with us, giving each of them a pair of shoes to show my appreciation for their hard work.

When my time was up, I was ready. Happiness and exhaustion washed over me—ice and fire both trickling down my arms as I breathed in deep and sunk into my airplane seat. It felt like a mission accomplished. By God, the trip was a success.

On my way out of the Congo, I looked down at my shoes atop the brown earth, worn and weathered. Once, this land was stained with blood, marred by violence, terror, and heartbreak. That day, the ground was scarred by fresh shoeprints. They were small, like my feet once were. I watched a boy, not unlike I was years ago, packing dirt as his legs carried him, faster, faster. He was laughing. In a way, that boy was me once. The tread patterns he left behind brought a promise of protection—however small—that he, and all the children in their new shoes, could only have dreamed of the night before. The ground was once a mat, stomped to the beat of my fear. But that day I was not running anymore. I heard a new song in the air as I listened to the patter of rubber on earth, of dust spraying against the wind. It was the sound of hope.

That hope rose up with me as I once again watched the African landscape disappear beneath a blanket of cloud, like snow on a perfect winter morning. This time, I wasn't running away. I was soaring on wings like an eagle's. God's strength filled me; His hope made me weightless.

I knew my work was far from done. But in my heart, hope was alighted, telling me that my own two eyes, the same ones that watched my country fall into chaos and ruin, will see real, lasting change in the Congo. It may have been the end of this chapter, this story in my life, but I was hopeful. This was only the beginning.

Afterword
Forgotten People
Today

History texts have said that the Second Congo War ended in 2003. But pockets of violence still erupt to this day, plaguing the Eastern Congo. Her people have been ravaged—bloodshed, kidnapping, and rape have made these people, my people, view the wealth of their land as a curse. I saw the fresh wounds with my own eyes: orphans, rape victims, child soldiers, destitute conditions. Like I said earlier in this book, everyone carries a piece of the Congo in their pocket. Yet, the Congolese are no better off for it. The same people who have been in power since our independence remain in power today. They are holding tightly to their seats, refusing to give up power, and don't work for

171

anyone but themselves. I have been privileged to have the opportunity to stand up and speak on behalf of the Congolese people.

I'm grateful that America welcomed me and my family when we were refugees. Coming here changed my life. I praise God for how He constructed my story to make me the person that I am today.

There is no doubt that God's hand was upon my family. When I look at how far God has brought me, I just want to thank Him. We are not better than those who did not make it. It is only by His mercies that He had a plan for my family. I am so humbled to be alive today, to be used for God's purpose.

My parents used to say, "You will see the God that we serve." I have. And while being alive is a great feeling, it is also a little bit scary. There is so much work to be done. When people were running after our family with knives, machetes, and guns, God overpowered all of that. He truly showed up and saved us, like He saved the Israelites from Pharaoh's hand. Like He saved Daniel from the lions' mouths. Like He saved Shadrach, Meshach, and Abednego from the flames.

When all hell broke loose in the Congo, my family escaped. I left behind family, friends, and loved ones, but I made new relationships here in the U.S., and for that I am grateful. I never had to miss home because of the people here who made America home to me.

I've lived the refugee life. I know how difficult it is. For all the refugees out there who fled persecution in their native lands, who seek a better life for their families, and right now are just waiting for an opportunity, I want to encourage you not to give up yet. There is hope. I pray that doors will open up for you.

As a refugee, there was nothing I could do about my circumstances. I was not able to look back or think about the suffering that my countrymen had to endure. As a man, cradled in a peaceful environment, I was almost too quick to forget. I no longer feared for my family to be dragged into the streets and murdered. I don't stay up at night worried someone will burst through the door to rape my sisters. I am no longer hungry, and I've been educated—but I must never forget. God keeps reminding me where I came from.

My two return trips to the Congo that I chronicled here in this book are my ever-present reminders of what God has called me to and why the Ntibonera Foundation exists—to share the love of Christ and to provide relief to those who need it most, those who have been forgotten.

Since 1996, the Congo has endured a silent holocaust. More than six million people have died. No one can know the exact number as so many of these atrocities have taken place deep in the jungle villages where there is no communication with the outside world. Even today, people are dying like flies. Women are raped every day.

When I heard about how rebels, evil men, would invade villages and rape every last woman and girl there, it made me sick. I could not believe the depths of depravity—just how twisted and evil men have become. Anyone who resisted was killed. My own ears have heard parents cry out for daughters who were kidnapped and never returned. Some who are kidnapped are raped over and over until the rebels finally kill them; others are forced to stay and serve as their wives. To this day, there are parents who are still looking for their children lost all those years ago.

Congo has been called the rape capital of the world, with an area at one time estimated to experience nearly fifty rapes per hour[13]. (Congolese women prefer "the world capital of sisterhood and solidarity," as *The Guardian* reported in 2017[14]. They choose to seize their own destiny rather than let the atrocities of the past define them.)

Whether young or old, no one is safe. A friend of my dad's, Dr. Denis Mukwege, started a hospital in Eastern Congo for rape victims. He has treated more than thirty thousand women. Dr. Mukwege has given care to girls as young as eight and to women who are grandmothers.

The extent of this is beyond reason. Women are raped on their way to market, out working the farm, and even in their own homes. Some are raped by more than five men at a time—I cannot believe how one could survive that sort of trauma or endure afterward. When I was in the Congo recently, I met a woman who was raped so badly that now she cannot even walk.

This evil has to be stopped.

Dr. Mukwege received a Nobel Prize in 2018 for his work saving the women of the Congo—I'm thankful there are people like him trying to restore lives and hope in my motherland.

The Congolese people have been forgotten for so long.

Due to a corrupt government, the Congolese have never enjoyed the country that God has blessed them with. While minerals make the land among the world's wealthiest, the Congo continues to be one of the poorest nations in the world. The same regime has been in power for fifteen years and refuses to step aside. Most of these government officials have permanent residences outside of the Congo. They hold power to enrich themselves, and then remove themselves far away from the country's problems.

The Congolese are tired of no one being willing to stand up for their interests. They want to elect their own leaders. To get the peace they have been longing for, my people need free and fair elections.

It is time for change.

Congo's wealth has been exploited for more than a century. Profiteers, militant rebels, and even our neighboring nations have battled for control over resources to which they have no claim. The countries that have been suspected of supporting rebels to profit off of the Congo's resources must put an end to that. No one should enrich themselves at the expense of others. And the Congolese who have become embittered toward neighbors from these nations must learn to forgive. Both sides must learn to live in peace.

My people say their country is cursed; they wish the Congo had no minerals at all. That's because the wealth it brings others is at the expense of Congolese blood, shed daily.

About sixty percent of the world's cobalt[15] comes from the Congo. And as much as eighty percent of the world's coltan is found there[16]. This precious metal is used in all of our modern electronics—phones, computers, laptops, gaming consoles, tablets—and for aerospace and military defense, including jet engines. Congo is so important to the world's technology and yet the country itself is desperately in need of modern infrastructure, proper healthcare, even basic necessities.

All of the things that we enjoy every day are paid for in lives every day. Five-year-olds are put to work in mines. The work is hard enough for a man but unthinkable for a child, and yet tens of thousands of Congolese kids are involved in every stage of cobalt mining. The latest research by the United Nations Children's Fund (UNICEF) estimates there are *forty thousand* children working the DRC mines. These kids spend most of the day breathing in toxic fumes.

Child soldiers battle over the profits of our excess. Abducted kids, hardly old enough to go to school, have guns thrust in their hands and are forced to kill. The men who profit sexually abuse women for their own sick pleasure and to excise power and instill fear. Congolese men have failed the people, so I believe it is time for women and young people to step up to the plate and reclaim their country from its long-term, corrupt leaders. I plan to help educate young Congolese people to have a positive outlook on life and to bring that hope into the government, rising as new leaders who will truly serve the nation's interests.

I want the world to understand what is going on in the Congo, to know the true price behind the tag on the shelf. We must remember these forgotten people. No one should have to die or suffer for these electronic gadgets.

Sometimes I ask myself how many millions have to die for the world to know.

My people are tired of war. They want to live in peace. America, you have done so much for me, and I am forever grateful. I was a stranger and you let me in, you gave me a chance to better myself and my family. I am not the person I once was. You helped me recognize myself. Thank you. This truly is the Land of Opportunity where everyone has a chance. Now, I am asking for you to stand with me, like so many already have with the Ntibonera Foundation, and help amplify the Congolese voice.

I know that you, dear reader, wherever you are, can help be the solution to this problem. Share this story with your friends, your family, your neighbors, your community, your church. Reach out to members of Congress, key government officials who can help advocate for change in the Congo. Let's fight for peace in the Democratic Republic of the Congo. Let's show the world that we do not side with exploitation, oppression, and injustice and will not stand for a regime in the Congo that will allow those things, explicitly or through indifference. Together, We Stand With Congo.

Know that the profits from this book are being put to work for the Congo. The trips you read about were only the beginning. When I was in the DRC, I witnessed with my own eyes the spark that can set ablaze a light that will drive out the darkness that plagues my motherland. Something so simple as the excess of our closets, the neglected footwear and apparel, can help to transform lives. And as my work grows, we will build schools, ensure orphanages and hospitals are properly funded, and strive to give the Congolese the dignity they deserve.

One of the long-term goals of the Ntibonera Foundation is to build a center that includes a hospital, a library, and a school for child soldiers, orphans, Pygmies, the children born as a result of rape, and impoverished children from underprivileged communities. The school will emphasize entrepreneurial skills, encouraging these people to go out and start their own businesses. We will have trade schools—carpentry, sewing—to give people skills that will give them hope for a brighter future. We will help women take back their lives after being abused. The center will also have places for recreation and community building: basketball and tennis courts, soccer fields, and a track. We plan to make the library open to the public. For that project, we need to secure about five acres of land.

Once the center is completed, we then plan to expand our outreach, building more schools across the country, educating ethical leaders who have integrity, and investing in women's empowerment initiatives. This education will lead to grassroots efforts focused on peace, reconciliation, hope, and justice. We believe that the future of the DRC—my country, my home—is in those for whom the war and evil men tried to destroy.

The Ntibonera Foundation will continue in its mission to ensure that no child in the Congo, or the whole of Africa, has to stop going to school because they do not have shoes and are afraid to walk on contaminated soil. We will work to provide for every last child. And we will fight for justice and the protection of human rights; we will not cease fighting as long as kids are being used as soldiers.

I saw the beginning with my own eyes—a pair of shoes was a symbol of hope to the Congolese. Together, let's show them what hope can bring.

If you would like to support the Ntibonera Foundation or learn more about us, visit NtiboneraFoundation.org or contact us at info@ntibonerafoundation.org. The Ntibonera Foundation appreciates your partnership. To inquire or support by mail, write to:

Ntibonera Foundation
1852 Banking Street
Greensboro, NC 27408

Acknowledgements

The Authors Would Like to Thank:

Foremost, all thanks and glory to God, the true author of this story.

This book would not have been possible without the tremendous support of Liberty University, for inspiring and educating each of us, for bringing us together, and for its commitment to a global mission and to empowering future leaders in every corner of society. Thank you to Jerry Falwell Jr., David Nasser, all of the university leadership, and for the student body and alumni family who supported the work we are doing.

We are extremely grateful to Scott Lamb for believing in us, sharing his industry knowledge, and for helping this story make it to print.

Stephen and Ayesha Curry—thank you for believing in the mission and for lending your time and energy to the cause. Your generosity has lit up countless faces of little boys and girls in the Congo.

Thanks to Chris Strachan for his incredible support and boundless joy and energy. You are our brother. We appreciate everyone with Kick'n It. Keep up the incredible work, and thank you for partnering with us.

To David Hancock, Terry Whalin, Margo Toulouse, Nickcole Watkins, Amber Parrott, and the team at Morgan James, thanks for bringing this book to the world. It was a pleasure working with you—all of your expertise and hard work has meant the world to us. Thank you Rachel Lopez for the incredible cover design.

Our wonderful editor, Mitzi Bible, helped to clean and sharpen this story. Thank you for your keen eye and guidance.

Finally, every single one of you readers, from the bottom of our hearts, God bless you. Thank you for coming along on this journey. We hope you feel inspired and empowered to work, in your own way, to help make the world a better place.

Emmanuel Would Also Like to Thank:

To the Ntibonera Foundation board of directors—Bret and Laurie Grieves and Janet Holbrook—thank you for believing in our vision. We appreciate you all for all the work you do.

It takes connections and resources to make an impact at the level the Ntibonera Foundation was able to (and continues to), and this work would not be possible without all of our generous partners. Thank you to Gleaning for the World, Under Armour, Nike, and our new partner: Samaritan's Purse. You are all changing the world.

To all of the supporters of the foundation and shoe drives over the years: thank you, thank you, thank you. There are no words to express the full extent of how much your help has meant to the Congo.

Drew, thank you for working with me to bring my story into the light. You are amazing bro; it was an honor working with you. You became family, a big brother through the whole process. I appreciate you very much.

Last but not least, I would like to acknowledge with gratitude the support and love of my family—my parents, Vincent and Martha, my brothers John, Baraka and Christian, my sisters Adili, Priscilla, Asi, Naomi and Esther. Thank you all for allowing me to share our story. This would not have been possible without you.

Drew Would Also Like to Thank:

Emmanuel, thank you for trusting me to help me tell your story. This work is bigger than me and beyond anything I ever dreamed I could be a part of. This has been a wild journey and I appreciate you bringing me along. I've gained another brother.

Naomi—I couldn't ask for a more incredible partner on this life adventure. Boys, you mean the world to me. My family, Mom, Dad, Aaron, Jessica, Zac plus Alisha, Matt, Evonne, all my nieces and nephews, Grandma Mock and Grandpa Don, my in-laws, Lewis and Karen, and each of my aunts uncles, and cousins: love you all and thanks for your prayers and support.

To all of the early readers and supporters of this story, thanks so, so much for your assistance. Diane Austin, Melissa Webb, Jen Redmond, Ana Campbell, Bobby Simon, Andrew Trowbridge, Ashlee and Jason Glen, and Debra Torres: I'm grateful for your insight and encouragement from the book's infancy.

I could certainly thank countless more of you, and I apologize that I cannot list each of you by name, but know that I recognize I wouldn't be where I am today without you.

About the Authors

Emmanuel Ntibonera is a gifted public speaker, humanitarian at heart, and a singer/songwriter who has built a successful non-profit—the Ntibonera Foundation, which shares the love of Christ while bringing hope and relief to those suffering in the Congo and in Africa as a whole—from the ground up. Through his efforts, he has secured fundraising, booked gigs across the country, and raised ten thousand pairs of shoes through sheer dedication. Emmanuel enjoys playing soccer, traveling, and leading worship with his family band while raising awareness about the issues Congolese people face. He graduated from Liberty University with a bachelor's degree in health promotion and an MBA. Emmanuel was born in the Democratic Republic of the Congo and then moved to Kenya, where he lived as a refugee after his family was forced to flee their home due to war and political instability. He lives in Greensboro, North Carolina.

Drew Menard is a professional writer living in Charlotte, NC, with his wife and four active boys. He earned a bachelor's degree in journalism and a master's in strategic communication from Liberty University, where he published his thesis on the emergent trend of transmedia storytelling. Drew is an award-winning columnist who has written extensively for magazines, newspapers, and digital publications. His creative projects also include developing screenplays and novels.

Endnotes

1   The Editors of Encyclopaedia Britannica, "Mobutu Sese Seko," Encyclopaedia Britannica, Dec. 6, 2016, https://www.britannica.com/biography/Mobutu-Sese-Seko.

2   World Atlas, 2017

3   Worldometers, 2017

4   UN World Population Prospects, 2017

5   "Q&A: DR Congo conflict," *BBC News*, Nov. 20, 2012, http://www.bbc.com/news/world-africa-11108589.

6   "DR Congo: Cursed by its natural wealth," *BBC News*, Oct. 9, 2013, http://www.bbc.com/news/magazine-24396390.

7   "Rwanda Genocide: 100 Days of Slaughter," *BBC News*, April 7, 2014, https://www.bbc.com/news/world-africa-26875506.

8   Mollie Zapata, "Congo: The First and Second Congo Wars, 1996-2003," *Enough Project*, November 29, 2011, https://enoughproject.org/blog/congo-first-and-second-wars-1996-2003.

9   The true death toll is unknown as limited access made it difficult for organizations to investigate the fallout.

10 *MedLinePlus.gov*, June 4, 2018, https://medlineplus.gov/ency/ article/001604.htm

11 "Deal to end Kenyan crisis agreed," *BBC News*, April 12, 2008, http://news.bbc.co.uk/2/hi/africa/7344816.stm.

12 Nina Strochlic, "Why Pygmies are dealing weed to survive," *National Geographic*, March 22, 2017, https://news. nationalgeographic.com/2017/03/democratic-republic-congo-pygmy-grow-deal-weed/.

13 Mark Townsend, "Revealed: how the world turned its back on rape victims of Congo," *The Guardian*, June 13, 2015, https://www. theguardian.com/world/2015/jun/13/rape-victims-congo-world-turned-away.

14 Justine Masika Bihamba, "The 'rape capital of the world'? We women in Congo don't see it that way," *The Guardian*, October 9, 2017, https://www.theguardian.com/global-development/2017/ oct/09/the-rape-capital-of-the-world-we-women-in-democratic-republic-congo-dont-see-it-that-way.

15 Todd C. Frankel, "The Cobalt Pipeline," *The Washington Post*, September 30, 2016, https://www.washingtonpost.com/graphics/ business/batteries/congo-cobalt-mining-for-lithium-ion-battery/?noredirect=on.

16 Kathy Feick, "Coltan," *University of Waterloo Earth Sciences Museum*, https://uwaterloo.ca/earth-sciences-museum/resources/ detailed-rocks-and-minerals-articles/coltan.